# Teach Someone to READ

## A Step-by-Step Guide for Literacy Tutors

Including Diagnostic Phonics
and Comprehension Assessments

**Nadine Rosenthal**

Director, Center for Reading Improvement
San Francisco State University

Reading Consultant/Tutor Trainer
California Literacy Campaign

Fearon Education
a division of
David S. Lake Publishers
Belmont, California

*For my adult literacy students—*
*who continually teach me*
*what learning is all about*

*Cover photograph by Michael Falconer*

ISBN 0-8224-5834-9

Printed in the United States of America

10 9 8 7 6 5 4 3 2

1330277

WEST KILDONAN

# Contents

# PART 1

*Introduction*

# *Introduction*

*Teach Someone to Read* was written with two goals in mind. The first goal was to give new tutors who are not professional teachers some techniques for teaching others to read and write. The second goal was to help new tutors approach their task with a thorough understanding of the meaning of literacy in its broadest sense.

The tutoring techniques presented in *Teach Someone to Read* focus on the needs and interests of adult and adolescent students. Teaching literacy skills to people with substantial life experience is quite different from teaching basic reading skills to young children. Teachers of the young generally teach word recognition intensively through second grade. Comprehension is taught only later, when the children are deemed old enough to comprehend. From the beginning, however, older students can rely on their understanding of the meanings of words in order to recognize them.

Adults and adolescents who are poor readers have personal histories of being defensive about and covering up their reading disabilities. The techniques recommended here help to eliminate such barriers to learning and replace inhibition and anxiety with interest and enthusiasm. In summary, the techniques are as follows:

1. Assess your student's needs and develop comprehension and word-recognition activities based on those needs.

2. Integrate those activities into readings on topics of strong personal interest to your student.

3. Discuss and analyze the readings while using them as the context for additional comprehension, word recognition, and writing activities.

These techniques are easy to implement in a one-to-one tutorial relationship. They can also be readily adapted for use with small groups of students. Junior high school, high school, and adult basic education remedial reading teachers can use these techniques to enhance their lessons as well.

*Teach Someone to Read* develops the premise that literacy in its entirety includes the critical thinking and analytical skills that allow people to function productively in society. When literacy is viewed in this light, a tutor's task is shown to be more than teaching basic word-recognition and writing skills. That task is to integrate instruction in these basic skills with instruction in the skills needed to comprehend, interpret, analyze, criticize, and act upon the words recognized. It also implies the need to place all these skills into a context that is meaningful to the student.

# A Comprehension-Based Literacy Training Program

*Literacy means more than being able to read and write words. It means taking meaning from print and giving meaning to print.*

*Teach Someone to Read* utilizes a comprehension-based approach to literacy training. The assumption behind this approach is that there is little reason for people to learn to read and write unless the words they learn are connected to facts and ideas that are important for them to comprehend. In such a meaningful context, learning to read the actual words of a text turns into a straightforward process. Students use their prior knowledge of the subject and context clues to predict what words might come next. Then they figure out the pronunciation of the words using phonics and syllabication rules.

This comprehension-based approach to literacy training is significantly different from other methods. Other methods tend to teach phonics primarily by using word lists, workbooks, flash cards, and texts with controlled vocabularies. Comprehension is generally taught later by having the student read materials that bear on day-to-day living—bus schedules, prescriptions, directions, warranties, and so forth—or stories with high interest but low reading levels. On the other hand, this comprehension-based method stresses the teaching of phonics *within* the framework of readings that are of particular interest to the student. Word lists, flash cards, and other phonics reinforcement activities are used as supplementary materials.

## Elements of the Program

In Part 1 of the guide, a variety of background information on illiteracy is presented. This part also gives some guidelines that will be useful for you as a new tutor. Parts 2 and 3 contain the main elements of the program. Part 2, "Diagnostic Testing," comprises two diagnostic assessments. The Rosenthal Diagnostic Phonics Assessment (RDPA) helps you to assess your student's strengths and weaknesses in recognizing phonically regular words. The Rosenthal Diagnostic Comprehension Assessment (RDCA) helps you to determine your student's ability to read short selections and comprehend the meaning of their content. Both assessments are easy to administer and interpret.

Part 3, "Read to Learn, Learn to Read," is the very heart of the program itself. Essentially, it forms a manual of useful tutoring techniques. The first chapter sets forth guidelines for planning your lessons. You learn to develop lesson plans that allow you to teach word skills in a context that is of personal interest to your student. The next chapter focuses on comprehension development—reading to learn. The emphasis here is on personalizing the reading process so that your student will be highly motivated to learn. It shows you how to select reading topics and to find appropriate reading materials on those topics. Then it tells you how to expand the topics, question your student to improve comprehension, train the student to ask his or her own questions, and teach study skills. The final chapter focuses on word recognition—learning to read. Here you learn the methods for teaching basic reading and writing skills. The methods presented include the sight-word, phonics, syllabication, and language-experience techniques. Other skills fundamental to the reading process—vocabulary, spelling, and writing skills—are also addressed here. A variety of development and reinforcement activities for each skills area is included.

Part 4, "Teaching Resources," tells you how to obtain information about literacy programs and gives a list of reference materials for literacy tutors. A list of publishers of reading materials suitable for literacy students is also provided. As a handy synopsis of many of the techniques presented in the guide, the Checklist Reviews from Chapters 2 and 3 of Part 3 are duplicated here. A discussion of non-standard English completes the guide.

# Background on Illiteracy

*If you cannot read, you probably have low self-esteem. Without self-esteem, you cannot learn to read.*

We read to learn—and thus to grow. With growth comes the ability to see new things and to see old things in new ways. That ability, in turn, gives us the power to control our lives by making changes that were previously unimaginable. Literacy, then, leads us to more than a simple grasp of written words. It leads us to more meaningful lives.

## How Much Illiteracy Is There?

National statistics on illiteracy are staggering. They depict a dire educational situation in this country.

National literacy statistics look at "functional literacy." Someone who is functionally literate has the reading and writing skills necessary for everyday living—for reading labels, ads, directions, bus schedules, TV guides, and warranties. Functionally literate people can also fill in job application forms, write letters, and perform simple work procedures. Those who are able to function at this basic level are assumed to have a reading ability at the fourth-grade level.

Conservative estimates reveal that there are about 25 million adult Americans who are functionally illiterate. That is nearly one-tenth of the nation's population. Add to that another 45 million adults who are only marginally literate—who read and write at only a junior-high-school level—and the total rises to more than 70 million. This group comprises more than a quarter of the population. Although the largest number of illiterate adults is whites, the percentages for blacks, Native Americans, and Hispanics are much higher. Sixteen percent of adult whites, 44 percent of adult blacks, 54 percent of adult Native Americans, and 56 percent of adult Hispanics are functionally or marginally illiterate. Overall the national high school dropout rate is 27 percent. But again, the percentages for blacks, Native Americans, and Hispanics are considerably higher than the average rate.

## What Are the Costs to Society?

The costs to society of such widespread illiteracy are immense. It is estimated that 15 percent of the nation's work force is functionally illiterate. Lowered production due to errors, accidents, and high turn-over rates—often attributable to illiteracy—results in losses of hundreds of billions of dollars a year. Of the people who are chronically unemployed, 75 percent are functionally illiterate. Thus, the nation's welfare and unemployment payments can also be related directly to our high illiteracy rates.

Prison operation costs the United States about $7 billion annually. Functionally illiterate prisoners account for 50 percent of the prison population, while 75 percent of all prisoners have not completed high school. A more alarming statistic reveals that 85 percent of all juvenile delinquents are considered functionally illiterate.

Illiteracy is also closely related to health-care issues. Due to inadequate health-care insurance and poorer health-care management, undereducated people suffer in comparison with educated people. Their life expectancies are shorter, their infant mortality rates are higher, and their illnesses are more frequent and lengthier. Under-educated people, therefore, lose more work and wages because of their illnesses.

The societal costs of illiteracy can be measured in neatly imper-sonal statistics. The personal costs, however, are much more difficult to calculate. There are no measurable gauges for the poor self-esteem, anxiety, and sense of failure that undereducated people feel when confronting many life situations.

## What Are Some of the Causes?

The United States is an extremely wealthy nation. It boasts some of the finest universities and some of the greatest minds in the world. Yet despite our wealth, resources, and talents, we are incapable of adequately educating nearly a third of our people. We can't educate about a tenth of them at all. The causes of such a high illiteracy rate are necessarily complex, but several factors are readily apparent. Any one of them might cause a growing child to react by not being able to learn to read.

ENVIRONMENTAL FACTORS

### Case Study

*Casey is 45 years old. When he signed up for tutoring in basic reading, he didn't know what a vowel was. He talked openly about the responsibilities he'd had as a child. As the oldest of five children of a single working mother, he was heavily burdened with household duties at an early age. At school he was too tired to concentrate and often fell asleep in his chair. By the time he was in the fourth grade, Casey was already two grades below level. He tried very hard, but he was never able to catch up.*

■  ■  ■

Casey's childhood is one example of a home environment that diverted energies away from learning. In other situations, the parent or parents might be overworked, underpaid, underemployed, unemployed, workaholic, alcoholic, drug-addicted, disabled, mentally unstable, depressed, angry, or hostile. The families might move frequently for jobs or housing or because of separation, divorce, or marriage. Parents might be verbally, physically, or sexually abusive to each other or to their children. Either or both of the parents might also be poor readers.

Peer pressure to cut school, use drugs, or get involved in petty crime is another factor that might sidetrack a youth away from learning. The ability to resist such pressure takes a singlemindedness that many young people are not capable of.

Television can also be classified as an environmental roadblock to learning. It creates images for the viewers rather than requiring them to create their own. Therefore, many people who are addicted to television find it difficult to think about and visualize the words they read. Often, television programs also take the place of parents reading to their young children. This is an activity that is important to the development of an appreciation for printed words.

PSYCHOLOGICAL FACTORS

### Case Study

*Suzanne is a 38-year-old grandmother. She recently enrolled in adult school to learn the basic reading skills she never picked up in high school. She described her thoughts while reading like this: "It's like I'm driving a car that has just stalled on a busy street, and everyone is looking at me. The more I hurry, the more I panic, and then I can't ever get it going. It's the same way with reading for me. I get so nervous that I just can't read."*

■    ■    ■

It is extremely difficult for poor readers to reverse their histories of frustration, trauma, and failure with reading. They often become very anxious while trying to read, especially when they are asked to read aloud. Their anxiety may cause them to block the words even before they begin to sound them out.

Some poor readers become experts in creating defense mechanisms and in manipulating family, work, and social situations in order to avoid reading. But continual cover-ups and manipulations create incredible stress. That stress further erodes the poor reader's already low self-esteem.

Without self-esteem, poor readers have great difficulty developing the confidence necessary to take actions that will improve their lives.

Instead, they may hold in their frustrations and become depressed, or they may take their frustrations out indirectly on other people or on property. They may even rely on others to make their decisions for them.

## EDUCATIONAL FACTORS

*Case Study*

> *Greg is a very bright 20-year-old. He can read almost any word put in front of him, but he understands almost nothing he reads. He can talk about the general subject of an article, but he can't deal with the specific details in it.*
>
> *Greg talks with frustration about his school years. In class he was told over and over again that he had to read the books the other students were reading. But these books made no sense to Greg: the wording was stiff, and the content had little to do with his own life. Although he refused to read those books, he was given no chance to work with other materials. So Greg is still unable to understand written words.*

■   ■   ■

Many students are not able to relate to the standard controlled-vocabulary readers that most school systems offer. Without reading materials that are relevant to their lives, such students see no reason to learn to read at all.

Another problem in school is the emphasis that many elementary teachers place on word-perfect oral reading skills over comprehension of the text. Students who are constantly corrected for mis-pronunciations can become so cautious about reading that they will sometimes just stop trying to read.

It is more difficult for speakers of nonstandard English, such as black English, to learn to read and write than it is for standard English speakers. Consequently, teachers sometimes expect less from these students. Teachers don't take the necessary steps to help these students participate in the learning situation. For a more thorough discussion of nonstandard English, see page 203 in Part 4 of this guide.

## PHYSICAL FACTORS

### Case Study

*Matt is a kind and thoughtful 25-year-old man who has been in adult beginning reading classes for two years. He consistently confuses single letters and their sounds. When asked to read the simplest of words, he is unsure how to begin. Matt has watched other beginning adult students progress. He is beginning to believe that no matter how hard he tries, he may never be able to read. His teacher thinks he should stick to learning a few basic important words by sight.*

■   ■   ■

Physical factors contributing to illiteracy include various constitutional and genetic disabilities. Children without access to quality health care can have undiagnosed physical disabilities. These may be caused by organic health problems or undernourishment. Excessive sugar or chemical intake can induce hyperactivity. Genetic disabilities include inherited vision, speech, hearing, and coordination problems.

Neurological disabilities are rare in the general population, but they do account for a small percentage of reading problems. These disabilities include brain injuries and epilepsy, as well as a variety of learning disabilities that are often referred to as "dyslexia."

Although dyslexia is a nonspecific condition, the term generally is applied to a set of specific reading problems related to physical and neurological disabilities. To be diagnosed as dyslexic, a person must satisfy the following conditions: 1) reading ability must be severely below grade level; 2) intellectual abilities must be obvious; 3) regular educational opportunities must have been made available; and 4) emotional, cultural, economic, environmental, and psychological factors must have been previously ruled out as major causes of the reading disability.

# What Does It Feel Like to Be Illiterate?

Read these paragraphs.

Too many parents believe that their children have dyslexia. Just because a seven-
year-old child confuses b with d and g
with p, these parents think something is wrong
with the child. When an innate cause of a
child's reading problem can be pointed to,
the parents feel that they don't have to
accept any blame for the problem.
Many parents have their children put
through a battery of tests to find out why
the children can't read. At the end of the
testing, one thing is certain: the children
believe that they can't read because something is wrong with them. As a result,
they might very well just give up trying.

Were you inclined to pass that copy by without reading it? Did you decide you couldn't read it and just give up? Did you struggle through the two paragraphs only to find that by the time you had finished them, you had lost their meaning? Did you confuse some letters or words with others? Did you find yourself pointing to words so you wouldn't lose your place? Did you feel stupid, frustrated, irritated, or angry? These are the feelings that literacy students face every time they pick up a newspaper, look at written directions, or open a book.*

*If you were totally confused by the backward writing, this is what it says:

Too many parents believe that their children have dyslexia. Just because a seven-year-old child confuses *b* with *d* and *g* with *p*, these parents think something is wrong with the child. When an innate cause of a child's reading problem can be pointed to, the parents feel that they don't have to accept any blame for the problem.

Many parents have their children put through a battery of tests to find out why the children can't read. At the end of the testing, one thing is certain: the children believe that they can't read because something is wrong with them. As a result, they might very well just give up trying.

Those of us who are literate are used to being able to understand print effortlessly. It is probably impossible for us to drive by a billboard without reading the words printed on it. Your student, however, does not enjoy this ease of reading. He or she must struggle just to recognize words. To understand those words in context with others takes even harder work. Is it any wonder, then, that some people have given up on reading many times in their lives?

# Starting Out

*When you first meet your
student, just say hello.*

A thoughtful study of *Teach Someone to Read* will prepare you to begin tutoring as soon as you have found a student. You may choose to tutor a parent, a neighbor, a student in an adult education program, or a junior-high or high-school student. You might also work in a literacy program offered by a local community college, high school, library, or nonprofit literacy organization. If you sign up to work in an ongoing project, you will receive the benefit of formal training and support from the sponsoring group. But formal training is not essential. Indeed, the best training is experience.

## Pointers for the New Tutor

Virtually all new tutors and teachers are unsure of themselves at first, regardless of the amount of training they have received. But before you know it, you will feel confident in your tutoring abilities. This will become especially true as you see your student respond positively to the learning experience you offer.

HANDLE YOUR DOUBTS AND FEARS

*Case Study*

*Jonathan was to meet his new adult literacy student, Vic, in a couple of days. He couldn't recall feeling more insecure about anything in a long time. As an overachiever, Jonathan was temporarily immobilized by a fear of being rejected by his underachieving student. Then, during the initial session, Vic stated that he almost didn't come because he was afraid that he wouldn't meet with Jonathan's approval. Jonathan assured Vic that everyone is afraid to attempt new and difficult tasks, and that the fear would pass as they got to know each other.*

■  ■  ■

Meeting a student for the first time is a tense experience for the new tutor. Beforehand, you will find yourself asking questions such as these: Will my student like me? How will I know if I'm teaching the right things? How will I know when I've pushed the student too far? Your self-doubts might tempt you to procrastinate. You may tell yourself that since you really don't know what you're doing, it might be best to delay tutoring until you have had more training . . . or more time to think about it . . . or . . .

These questions and fears are normal, even healthy. If you just take the tutorial relationship one step at a time, you will survive those initial qualms. And they will disappear soon after you begin getting to know your student.

## BE PREPARED TO CHANGE

### *Case Study*

*When Janet became Alicia's literacy tutor, she lacked confidence in her tutoring ability. As a result, she prepared a very formal lesson plan for each session. After a month of strict adherence to these plans, Janet sensed some resistance in Alicia and asked what was wrong. Alicia said that Janet reminded her of her father, a very formal man of whom she was terrified. He never displayed any warmth and always expected Alicia to do everything correctly.*

*Alicia's reaction took Janet completely by surprise. Although she had never thought of herself as an authority figure, she could see that she had been playing that role with Alicia. From that point on, Janet made her lessons less rigid. As an unexpected benefit, she herself began to feel more comfortable in the sessions and more confident in her teaching abilities.*

■    ■    ■

Being able to learn new things means being prepared to undergo some changes. Your student, who anticipates new opportunities as a result of learning to read and write, probably understands this require- ment very well. In order to pursue those new opportunities, it will be necessary for your student to cast aside part of his or her old self.

The tutorial process is a learning experience for you, too. It is inevitable that you will also undergo some changes. As you proceed, many of your assumptions about education, learning, and reading will be brought up for review. Many of your concepts about people from different cultures, races, religions, and economic backgrounds will change. Change is an uncomfortable process because it requires you to be open and vulnerable. If you are prepared for some changes, however, you can minimize the discomfort they cause. Then you can begin to look forward to new growth potential.

## AVOID THE INSENSITIVITY PITFALL

### *Case Study*

*When Marla began tutoring Ralph, it was immediately obvious that he could read fairly well. But he couldn't write complete sentences or spell most two-syllable words. Ralph made continual excuses to get out of writing, but Marla refused to hear them. She told him that she did not want alibis, and that he must write if he wanted to improve himself. Marla felt that her student was trying to manipu- late her.*

*After observing Ralph's behavior, however, and listening to his stories about work for several weeks, Marla finally understood the nature of his problem. Ralph was a boss at his workplace and was well respected by his coworkers. But he was aware that people are judged harshly because of their poor writing skills, so he had spent years covering up his inability to write. Now he was carrying these cover- ups over to his tutoring sessions. As Marla talked with*

*Ralph about his writing concerns, she realized that she should continue to push him to write, but also give him the opportunity to voice his fears.*

■  ■  ■

New tutors particularly are prone to being so caught up in their own concerns about their teaching ability that they forget to address their students' concerns. This insensitivity tends to aggravate the students' shaky confidence and helps to alienate them.

It is important for you to tune in to your student and to drop any preconceived notions about that person. Pay close attention to what he or she says and does in your sessions. Since your student has a history of failure in the learning environment, he or she will have a lot to say about why that failure took place. If you are sensitive to this history, you will gain considerable insight into the methods that will or will not work for him or her. As a consequence, the results of your student's learning task—and your teaching task—will be far more successful.

## USE STUDENT-CENTERED INSTRUCTION

### Case Study

*Nina told Nathan, her literacy tutor, that she had been robbed recently in an alley of her housing project. Immediately, Nathan got information on police protection. He wrote the material at Nina's reading level and developed a phonics lesson from the reading. When Nina appeared disinterested in the material, Nathan felt annoyed. Why hadn't she responded positively to his good planning? Hadn't he listened to her needs and acted from an understanding of those needs?*

*When he discussed the topic further with Nina, however, Nathan realized that he was teaching her what he had thought she needed to know rather than what she wanted to learn. Nathan listened to Nina and thought about her response; then he changed the topic to self-defense for women.*

■  ■  ■

In traditional teacher-centered instruction, the teacher—the expert in the field—lectures on the subject matter while the students take notes. The teacher asks questions only to elicit "correct" answers. Then the students memorize those answers for exams. While some students enjoy a teacher-centered learning environment and find it effective, others fail miserably in such a structured and impersonal learning situation. They are incapable of rapidly assimilating new information without some personal reference.

Your student is likely to be among those who react in this negative way. Therefore, in your tutorial relationship, it is essential to use a student-centered instructional method. After discovering what your student wants and needs to learn, you prepare lessons that focus directly on those matters. Rather than serving as a "learning dictator," you serve as a "learning facilitator." In this manner, you help to develop your student's own ideas.

Student-centered instruction also encourages independent thinking and learning instead of reinforcing your student's dependence on you. It focuses you on providing a supportive, respectful, and challenging learning environment in which your student relies more and more upon his or her own resources. The process of learning to read and write is intimately connected with taking control over one's own life. Thus, literacy tutoring is a matter of helping your student open the doors to his or her untapped potential.

## The First Tutorial Session

Because neither you nor your student knows what to expect, the first tutorial session is often the most difficult one. It is a good idea to plan it very carefully so that you and your student come away from it knowing what to expect of each other.

INTRODUCING YOURSELVES

*Case Study*

*Helen was afraid that she would alienate Michael, her new literacy student, if she probed too deeply into his back-round during their first session. She did decide, however, to ask him some direct questions about his reading abilities*

*and his past attempts at learning to read. To her amaze-
ment, Michael appeared to enjoy talking about his past
reading experiences and his expectations for their sessions.
Knowing all this prompted Helen to tell Michael what she
planned to accomplish. Both of them left their first session
with high hopes for future ones.*

■  ■  ■

The main goal of your first session is to get to know your student.
This is the time to learn about his or her educational background
and personal interests. You should be able to accomplish these
tasks in a one- to two-hour session.

Start off with introductions. Tell each other about yourselves.
Explain why you are there and find out why he or she is there. Try to
put your student at ease. Remember, your student is likely to be
more nervous than you.

It is important that your student have confidence in you. No one
wants to know that a tutor is insecure, nervous, or self-conscious. So
even though you don't have a lot of practical experience, present
yourself as someone who is well prepared and who knows what he
or she is doing. Be careful, though, not to promise results that will
later prove impossible to accomplish. Some basic rules for the first
session are these: Be honest. Be direct. Be yourself.

Ask questions to find out about your student's reading history
and expectations. Keep your questions open-ended, and ask only
one question at a time. Be sure to give your student plenty of time to
answer each question before jumping in with another one. Here are
some sample first-session questions. They will help you formulate
others of your own.

- How well do you read?
- What are some of the major difficulties you have with reading?
- Did your family members read when you were growing up?
- How did you spend your time as a child? What things were important to you?
- Why do you think you still have difficulty reading?
- What were some of the worst experiences you had in school?

- Who were your worst teachers? What did they do that made them so bad?
- What were some of the best experiences you had in school?
- Who were your best teachers? What did they do that made them so good?
- Have you been tutored in reading before? How did that go? Did you learn anything then that could help us now?
- Do you read anything at home or at work? What?
- Do you have any medical problems that might get in the way of your reading?
- What do people at home, or friends, think about your going back to learn to read?
- What do you expect from the tutoring sessions?
- Is there anything you'd like to ask me? I'll answer as well as I can.

## CHOOSE A READING TOPIC

*Case Study*

*When Chris first asked Ben what topics he wanted to read about, Ben said he would read anything Chris thought would help him. But Chris kept on asking Ben about his interests, and finally he learned that Ben was very concerned about the protection of wild animals. It had never occurred to Ben that a tutor might let him read about this. He thought he'd have to read uninteresting stories just as he'd always done in school. Ben told Chris that he now felt more confident than ever that, this time, he would really learn to read.*

■   ■   ■

Your next step is to find a topic that will stimulate your student's desire to read. Materials that spark your student's imagination will help to develop his or her critical thinking abilities.

Begin by asking what topics your student would like to read about. On pages 64–86 in Part 3, you will find an in-depth discussion on choosing and expanding reading topics. There is also a list of suggested topics that are suitable for adults and adolescents. If your student can't come up with a topic, read the list aloud until a few possibilities catch his or her interest. Then narrow those possibilities down to one.

OBTAIN A WRITING SAMPLE

*Case Study*

*During their initial session, Donna asked Mary Ann to write something about her children. She seemed very proud of them. Mary Ann looked at Donna as if she couldn't do it, but she said she would try if Donna would help her with the spelling. After ten minutes of deep concentration.and six words that needed spelling help, Mary Ann came up with three short, poorly constructed sentences. Donna read the sentences, commented on how interesting they were, and encouraged Mary Ann to talk about her difficulties with writing. A long conversation ensued. Donna learned some of the reasons why Mary Ann found writing so difficult. They decided that, over the next few months, Mary Ann would write some of the stories she had just told Donna—with Donna's help, of course.*

■   ■   ■

Next, get a writing sample from your student. Since you both need to know how to contact each other in case of cancellations, begin by asking your student to write his or her name and telephone number for you. In exchange, provide yours.

Then, if you think your student can write a sentence or a short paragraph, ask for a writing sample on the topic you have just discussed. You will learn a great deal from reading this sample. You will learn if your student can write at all, if he or she has a sense of sentence structure, and if his or her spelling is functional. Pages 171–186 in Part 3 will provide you with steps for correcting writing and spelling problems.

CLARIFYING FUTURE ARRANGEMENTS

*Case Study*

*When Mario didn't show up for his first tutorial session, Naomi called him to find out what had happened. He said that he had forgotten and made a doctor's appointment for that time. They agreed to meet the next week at the same time and place. Not wanting a repeat of the previous week's misunderstanding, Naomi called Mario the night before the session was to take place. He said he had forgotten again, but he promised to be there.*

*Mario seemed very relieved when the session went well. He even admitted that he was really too scared to come the last time. Naomi then suggested that they agree to continue meeting weekly for a month. At the end of the month, either one of them could end the sessions if he or she didn't like them. Mario seemed to feel that he could handle this short-term commitment.*

■   ■   ■

Close the first session by arranging when and where you will meet for future sessions. Discuss how long each session will run.

It's usually best to start with a short-term arrangement. For example, plan to meet each week for a month. At the end of that first month, assess together what you have accomplished and what the future tutoring commitment will be. Short-term agreements encourage both of you to "stick with it" for a while, without pushing for too long a commitment from either of you. If the relationship works out, terrific. But if it's unsatisfactory for either of you, there is a built-in release or an opportunity to make changes.

# PART 2

# Diagnostic Testing

# ☞ *Diagnostic Testing* ☜

The second tutorial session is the time for getting a clear picture of a student's reading abilities and disabilities. The simple tests provided in this part of *Teach Someone to Read* will identify a student's problems with word recognition and reading comprehension. They will also tell you at approximately what grade level he or she reads. Both tests were developed especially for use with adult and adolescent literacy students who read between the first- and sixth-grade levels. They were carefully designed to be administered in a one-to-one tutorial situation.

The Rosenthal Diagnostic Phonics Assessment (RDPA) is an informal test of a student's ability to read lists of progressively difficult but phonically regular words. The lists range from grade levels one to four. Besides the word lists, the test contains three evaluation forms and a summary sheet. The evaluation forms are used to record the exact word parts the student misses in his or her responses. The summary sheet is used to correlate and analyze the evaluation data. Using this summary sheet, you will be able to identify those phonics areas in which the student needs tutorial work. The RDPA may also be used to assess spelling abilities. To do this, you simply have the student spell the list words as you dictate them.

The Rosenthal Diagnostic Comprehension Assessment (RDCA) is an informal test of a student's ability to read and understand short selections. It consists of six readings written at progressively higher grade levels, from one to six. Each selection is followed by a set of comprehension questions. These questions assess a student's abilities to handle literal recall, interpretive, and active questions. Once you have determined a student's difficulties with answering these questions, you can use the results to plan lessons that focus on the specific areas of reading comprehension in which the student is weak.

Multiple copies of the RDPA and RDCA are available from the publisher in a separate 8-½" x 11" format.

# Rosenthal Diagnostic Phonics Assessment

## Administering the Reading of the Lists

The following three steps provide a simple method for using the RDPA to assess a student's ability to recognize phonically regular words.

1. Have the student read as many words as possible in lists 2, 3, and then 4 on page 26. (If he or she misses five of the first ten words on list 2, stop there. Ask the student to read list 1 by giving first the names and then the sounds of the alphabet letters.) Stop the test when the student makes ten errors on a list or becomes frustrated.

2. As the student works through each word list, note all the misreading errors in the appropriate column on the corresponding *RDPA Evaluation Form* on page 27, 28, or 29. These errors will comprise either mispronunciations, substitutions, or omissions. Write the mispronounced words phonetically as you hear them. Write the substitutions and omissions just as the student says them.

3. The student reads at the approximate grade level indicated by the number of the highest list on which he or she makes seven to ten errors. Fewer than seven errors means the student is reading above the grade level of that list and should be tested on the next higher one. More than ten errors means the student is reading below the grade level of that list.

SCORE INTERPRETATION CHART

| Score | Interpretation |
|---|---|
| Fewer than 7 errors | The student reads above the grade level of that list. |
| 7 to 10 errors | The student reads at the grade level of that list. |
| More than 10 errors | The student reads below the grade level of that list. |

## Analyzing the Test Results

Tell the student that you will analyze the test results after the session is over and will discuss them the next time you meet.

Before you begin your analysis, read the headings in the analysis charts on all three evaluation forms. Taken together, these headings represent the elements you will use to teach word recognition skills. The elements are as follows:

1. single consonants
2. short vowels
3. beginning and end blends
4. beginning- and end-consonant digraphs
5. long vowels with silent *e*
6. vowel combinations
7. vowels controlled by *r*, *l*, and *w*
8. prefixes
9. V̆C/CV syllables (rule: two consonants between two vowels—divided between the consonants with the first vowel short)
10. V̄/CV or V̆C/V syllables (rule: one consonant between two vowels—divided before the consonant with the first vowel long or divided after the consonant with the first vowel short)
11. endings

Now follow these five steps to analyze the student's reading of the word lists.

1. Use the analysis chart on each evaluation form to circle the original word elements the student misread. (Don't concern yourself with the elements that were substituted for the originals.) On the evaluation form for list 2, for example, if the original word was *win* and the student said "won" circle the *i* on the chart. If the original word was *print* and the student said "paint" circle both the *pr* and the *i*. Continue in this manner with the analysis charts for lists 3 and 4.

2. Add the circles in each column and record the subtotals and totals at the bottom of the page. Subtotal scores for list 2 indicate that words covering the same phonics elements are continued on list 3. Carry the subtotals for list 2 over to the subtotal section on the evaluation form for list 3.

3. Transfer the totals from the three evaluation forms to the *RDPA Summary Sheet* on page 30. Write the totals in the column headed Errors Made. If the number of errors made in a phonics area is higher than the number allowed for that area, remedial work is required.

4. Look back through the three evaluation forms to see which types of errors were made most frequently. Record the errors on the summary sheet under the column headed Areas with Most Errors.

5. Finally, in the column headed Three Areas Needing Most Remedial Work, note the three phonics areas in which you'll begin remedial instruction.

## Using the RDPA as a Spelling Test

You may also use the RDPA to assess a student's ability to spell phonically regular words. To do this, have the student write the words in lists 2, 3, and 4 on a separate sheet of paper after you have said each one and used it in a sentence. Transfer the misspelled words to the evaluation forms exactly as the student wrote them. Score the forms in the same manner as for the reading test. This assessment of spelling ability is only to help you identify spelling problems needing work during the tutorial sessions. It does not give you any indication of a student's grade level in spelling.

## RDPA LISTS

| 1 | 2 | 3 | 4 |
|---|---|---|---|
| a | ran | shade | summer |
| d | met | smoke | final |
| g | kid | preach | napkin |
| k | job | coast | taken |
| n | cup | slide | lemon |
| f | sad | trail | mitten |
| t | hem | mount | driven |
| w | win | grief | hotel |
| o | fox | stall | panic |
| b | lug | tray | pencil |
| e | plan | shone | demand |
| h | belt | clown | closet |
| m | trim | sneeze | content |
| p | pond | faith | stupid |
| y | club | marsh | punish |
| s | bath | scrape | admitted |
| j | sled | bright | honoring |
| c | film | shoot | devotion |
| q | chop | speech | vanishes |
| i | junk | thrive | possibly |
| l | flash | roach | recently |
| z | chest | thief | confuses |
| r | print | squirt | pretended |
| u | stomp | ground | approaches |
| x | chunk | spray | digestion |
| v | crash | gloom | refinishing |
| n | swept | stream | discredited |
| c | think | scold | misconstruction |
| m | cloth | flight | unwavering |
| g | thump | world | improbably |

# Analysis Chart

Student: _____

ster: _____

te: _____

| Word | Misread as | Beginning Consonants | Beginning Blends | Beginning Digraphs | Short a | Short e | Short i | Short o | Short u | End Consonants | End Blends | End Digraphs |
|------|-----------|------|------|------|------|------|------|------|------|------|------|------|
| ran | | r | | | a | | | | | n | | |
| met | | m | | | | e | | | | t | | |
| kid | | k | | | | | i | | | d | | |
| job | | j | | | | | | o | | b | | |
| cup | | c | | | | | | | u | p | | |
| sad | | s | | | a | | | | | d | | |
| hem | | h | | | | e | | | | m | | |
| win | | w | | | | | i | | | n | | |
| fox | | f | | | | | | o | | x | | |
| lug | | l | | | | | | | u | g | | |
| plan | | | pl | | a | | | | | n | | |
| belt | | b | | | | e | | | | | lt | |
| trim | | | tr | | | | i | | | m | | |
| pond | | p | | | | | | o | | | nd | |
| club | | | cl | | | | | | u | b | | |
| bath | | b | | | a | | | | | | | th |
| sled | | | sl | | | e | | | | d | | |
| film | | f | | | | | i | | | | lm | |
| chop | | | | ch | | | | o | | p | | |
| junk | | j | | | | | | | u | | nk | |
| flash | | | fl | | a | | | | | | | sh |
| chest | | | | ch | | e | | | | | st | |
| print | | | pr | | | | i | | | | nt | |
| stomp | | | st | | | | | o | | | mp | |
| chunk | | | | ch | | | | | u | | nk | |
| crash | | | cr | | a | | | | | | | sh |
| swept | | | sw | | | e | | | | | pt | |
| think | | | | th | | | i | | | | nk | |
| cloth | | | cl | | | | | o | | | | th |
| thump | | | | th | | | | | u | | mp | |
| ERROR TOTALS | | ▓▓▓ | | | | | | | | ▓▓▓ | | |
| ERROR SUBTOTALS (to carry over to list 3) | | | | | ▓▓▓ | | | | | | | |

# RDPA Evaluation Form
## List 3—Grade Level 3

*Analysis Chart*

Student: _____

Tester: _____

Date: _____

| Word | Misread as | Beginning Consonants | Beginning Blends | Beginning Digraphs | 3-Letter Blends | Long a, ai, ay | ea, ee, ie | Long i, igh | Long o, oa | oo, ou | Vowel with r, l, w | End Consonants | End Blends | End Digraphs |
|---|---|---|---|---|---|---|---|---|---|---|---|---|---|---|
| shade | | | | sh | | a | | | | | | d | | |
| smoke | | | sm | | | | | | o | | | k | | |
| preach | | | pr | | | | ea | | | | | | | ch |
| coast | | c | | | | | | | oa | | | | st | |
| slide | | | sl | | | | | i | | | | d | | |
| trail | | | tr | | | ai | | | | | | l | | |
| mount | | m | | | | | | | | ou | | | nt | |
| grief | | | gr | | | | ie | | | | | f | | |
| stall | | | st | | | | | | | | all | | | |
| tray | | | tr | | | ay | | | | | | | | |
| shone | | | | sh | | | | | o | | | n | | |
| clown | | | cl | | | | | | | | ow | n | | |
| sneeze | | | sn | | | | ee | | | | | z | | |
| faith | | f | | | | ai | | | | | | | | th |
| marsh | | m | | | | | | | | | ar | | | sh |
| scrape | | | | | scr | a | | | | | | p | | |
| bright | | | br | | | | | igh | | | | t | | |
| shoot | | | | sh | | | | | | oo | | t | | |
| speech | | | sp | | | | ee | | | | | | | ch |
| thrive | | | | | thr | | | i | | | | v | | |
| roach | | r | | | | | | | oa | | | | | ch |
| thief | | | | th | | | ie | | | | | f | | |
| squirt | | | | | squ | | | | | | ir | t | | |
| ground | | | gr | | | | | | | ou | | | nd | |
| spray | | | | | spr | ay | | | | | | | | |
| gloom | | | gl | | | | | | | oo | | m | | |
| stream | | | | | str | ea | | | | | | m | | |
| scold | | | sc | | | | | | | | ol | d | | |
| flight | | | fl | | | | | igh | | | | t | | |
| world | | w | | | | | | | | | or | | ld | |
| | ERROR TOTALS | | | | | | | | | | | | | |
| | ERROR SUBTOTALS (carried over from list 2) | | | | | | | | | | | | | |

28

# RDPA Evaluation Form

List 4—Grade Level 4

Student: _____

Tester: _____

Date: _____

## Analysis Chart

| Word | Misread as | Prefixes | Short Vowel V̆ C\C V Consonant Consonant Vowel | Long Vowel V̄ C V Consonant Vowel | Short Vowel V̆ C V Consonant Vowel | Endings |
|------|-----------|----------|------|------|------|---------|
| summer | | | sŭm /mer | | | |
| final | | | | fī / nal | | |
| napkin | | | năp / kin | | | |
| taken | | | | tā / ken | | |
| lemon | | | | | lĕm / on | |
| mitten | | | mĭt / ten | | | |
| driven | | | | | drĭv / en | |
| hotel | | | | hō / tel | | |
| panic | | | | | păn / ic | |
| pencil | | | pĕn / cil | | | |
| demand | | | | dē / mand | | |
| closet | | | | | clŏs / et | |
| content | | | cŏn / tent | | | |
| stupid | | | | stū / pid | | |
| punish | | | | | pŭn / ish | |
| admitted | | | ăd / mit | | | ted |
| honoring | | | | | hŏn / or | ing |
| devotion | | | | dē / vo | | tion |
| vanishes | | | | | văn / ish | es |
| possibly | | | pŏs / sib | | | ly |
| recently | | | | rē / cent | | ly |
| confuses | | | cŏn / fu | | | ses |
| pretended | | | | prē / tend | | ed |
| approaches | | | ăp / proach | | | es |
| digestion | | | | dī / ges | | tion |
| refinishing | | re | | | fĭn / ish | ing |
| discredited | | dis | | | crĕd / it | ed |
| misconstruction | | mis | cŏn / struc | | | tion |
| unwavering | | un | | wā / ver | | ing |
| improbably | | im | | | prŏb / ab | ly |
| | ERROR TOTALS | | | | | |

# RDPA Summary Sheet

Student: _____

Tester: _____

Date: _____

| Phonics Area Tested | Times Tested | Errors Allowed | Errors Made | Areas with Most Errors | Three Areas Needing Most Remedial Work |
|---|---|---|---|---|---|
| Beginning Consonants | 21 | 6 | | List errors | |
| Beginning Blends | 25 | 8 | | Circle:  Blends with  l  r  s | |
| Beginning Digraphs | 9 | 3 | | Circle:  sh  ch  th | |
| 3-Letter Blends | 5 | 2 | | List errors: | |
| Short Vowels | 30 | 9 | | Circle:  a  e  i  o  u | |
| Vowel Combinations | 18 | 5 | | Circle:  ai/ay  ea/ee/ie  igh  oa  oo/ou | |
| Vowel with r, l, w | 6 | 2 | | Circle:  r  l  w | |
| End Consonants | 33 | 10 | | List errors: | |
| End Blends | 15 | 4 | | Circle:  Blends with  l  n  m  p  s | |
| End Digraphs | 9 | 3 | | Circle:  sh  ch  th | |
| Vowel with Silent e | 7 | 2 | | Circle:  a  i  o | |
| Prefixes | 5 | 2 | | Circle:  re  dis  mis  un  im | |
| Syllables | 30 | 9 | | Circle:  $\breve{V}C/CV$  $\bar{V}/CV$  $\breve{V}C/V$ | |
| Endings | 15 | 4 | | Circle:  es  ed  ing  tion  ly | |

# Rosenthal Diagnostic Comprehension Assessment

## Administering the Reading Selections

To start the testing, choose the RDCA reading selection that you think will be fairly easy for the student to handle. If you have previously given the RDPA to the student, you can use the grade level determined by that test to make the first selection. (The grade level of a selection is indicated by its number.) Then if you judge the student able, move on to the next level of reading. Continue in this fashion until you reach the limit of his or her comprehension abilities. Be sure that you have read each selection you're planning to use before beginning your testing. It would be too difficult to read and comprehend the selections yourself during the testing situation.

The three steps below provide a straightforward approach to administering the reading selections.

1. Introduce the selection by briefly discussing its title. Tell the student that since you will be asking questions about the content, he or she should focus on what the reading is about.

2. Have the student read the selection aloud to you. If he or she stumbles over a word, allow a few seconds for self-correction and then pronounce it yourself. Remember, the point of the test is to determine reading comprehension abilities, not word recognition. But, if the student can't comprehend the reading because he or she is stumbling over numerous words, stop the reading and turn to an easier selection.

3. Make a list of the words the student misread and note the mispronunciation, substitution, and omission errors. Later, add these to the errors the student made on the RDPA so that you can do further phonics analysis on them.

## Asking the Questions and Evaluating the Answers

A set of comprehension questions follows each selection. Each set is divided into three categories, with two types of questions in each one. The questions are numbered consecutively, as follows:

■ Literal Recall Questions

1. Describe: observe, recall, state details, recognize facts
   The student is asked to describe information stated explicitly in the selection.
2. Reorganize: translate, paraphrase, summarize, classify, categorize, recognize main ideas
   The student is asked to reorganize the information and ideas stated explicitly in the selection into his or her own words.

■ Interpretive Questions

3. Analyze: interpret, infer, synthesize, compare, contrast
   The student is asked to analyze ideas that go beyond those stated explicitly in the selection in order to extract deeper meaning.
4. Generalize: evaluate, judge, conclude, conceptualize, form opinions, take a stand
   The student is asked to take the information and ideas already described and analyzed and generalize from them to broader issues.

■ Active Questions

5. React: respond, react emotionally, make value judgments, appreciate
   The student is asked to react personally and emotionally to any feeling brought up in the selection.
6. Act: change, do
   The student is asked to tell how he or she could act on thoughts and feelings about the selection.

Follow the four steps below to ask the questions and evaluate the answers. No answer key is provided since the answers are either obvious or they are interpretive and not able to be judged as correct or incorrect. Since it is you who must decide if the responses are thorough and to the point, the scoring/rating system is subjective. It is better, then, to make an immediate judgment on the quality of an answer rather than to try to remember it for later evaluation. You will also want to discuss each selection with the student. This will let you get some notion of his or her ability to apply the selection's information and ideas to his or her own life.

1. After the student has finished reading a selection, take it away. Then ask the comprehension questions. (Also ask any follow-up questions that come to your mind.) Five numbers (5, 4, 3, 2, 1) appear to the right of each question in section A of the RDCA Selection Question Sheet. Score each answer on a scale of 5 to 1 by circling the appropriate number. Good equals 5 or 4 points, fair 3 points, and poor 2 to 1 points. A score in the 3 to 5 range means that the student can read, comprehend, and interpret at the grade level of the selection.

2. Add the two numbers you circled to the right of the literal recall questions. Write this combined score in the space provided in section B of the question sheet. Score the interpretive and active questions in section A in the same way.

3. Use the small chart in section C of the question sheet to find the rating for each of the three scores. Write the ratings in the spaces provided.

4. Go back to the next lower selection if the literal recall and interpretive ratings are poor. Stop here if the literal recall and interpretive ratings are fair. Continue to the next higher selection if the literal recall and interpretive ratings are good. You may also continue, regardless of rating, if the student was able to read the words easily or wants to continue. (Note: The active rating is not used to determine grade level. The active questions are used solely to determine the student's ability to act or react to the selection.)

SCORE/RATING INTERPRETATION CHART

| Score/Rating | Interpretation |
|---|---|
| Score: 8 to 10 points<br>Rating: Good | Good literal recall, interpretation, or active thinking at this grade level. The student can read this level of material independently. *The reading level of the selection is too low for your tutoring sessions. Offer more difficult reading.* |
| Score: 5 to 7 points<br>Rating: Fair | Fair literal recall, interpretation, or active thinking at this grade level. The student should be able to read this level of material with your help. *This selection is at the correct reading level to use in your tutoring sessions.* |
| Score: 2 to 4 points<br>Rating: Poor | Poor literal recall, interpretation, or active thinking at this grade level. The student cannot handle this level of material, even with help. *The reading level of the selection is too difficult for your tutoring sessions. Use easier readings.* |

## Looking for a Job

I need a job. I need one badly. But I'm tired of looking. Do you know what it's like? You get up each day. You get dressed. You take the bus to the job. You are asked to fill out a form. Or you are asked to read something. You can't do it. You don't know how to read. You can't write. So you say, "Thanks for your time." Then you go. You may go home. Or you may go to a bar. You should go to school. And you know it. But that's too hard. Too bad there's no easy way to learn how to read.

RDCA Selection 1

RDCA Question Sheet
    Selection 1—Grade Level 1

*Looking for a Job*

Student: _____

Tester: _____

Date: _____

A. Ask each question. Then circle a number to the right of the question to score the answer.

| Literal Recall Questions | Good | | Fair | | Poor |
|---|---|---|---|---|---|
| 1. What does this person want to do in an easy way? | 5 | 4 | 3 | 2 | 1 |
| 2. What happens when this person goes looking for a job? | 5 | 4 | 3 | 2 | 1 |

Interpretive Questions

| | | | | | |
|---|---|---|---|---|---|
| 3. Does this person really want to find a job? How can you tell? | 5 | 4 | 3 | 2 | 1 |
| 4. Should an employer judge a person's job skills by his or her ability to read and write? Why or why not? | 5 | 4 | 3 | 2 | 1 |

Active Questions

| | | | | | |
|---|---|---|---|---|---|
| 5. What advice would you give the person in the story? | 5 | 4 | 3 | 2 | 1 |
| 6. Would you take your own advice? Why or why not? | 5 | 4 | 3 | 2 | 1 |

B. Add the circled numbers for each pair of questions to derive three combined scores.

Literal Recall Score: _____

Interpretive Score: _____

Active Score: _____

C. Use this chart to find the rating for each combined score.

> Good = 8 to 10 points
> Fair = 5 to 7 points
> Poor = 2 to 4 points

Literal Recall Rating: _____

Interpretive Rating: _____

Active Rating: _____

STOP HERE if the literal recall and interpretive ratings are fair or poor. CONTINUE if the literal recall and interpretive ratings are good.

# Late for Work

The day started out all wrong. Pam's son didn't want to go. He kept playing with his toys. "I've got to get out of here," she told him. "My new hospital job won't wait for you."

They left the house at last. Pam was only ten minutes late. She took her son to his baby-sitter's house. Then she rushed to the bus stop. She paced back and forth. The bus was late. She looked at her watch. Time was slipping by. Then the bus came.

Pam got to the hospital and found the right floor. She took a deep breath and then walked up to the head nurse.

"You're the new nurse's aide?" the head nurse asked. "You're late. It's 7:20. Be on time from now on, or you won't be working here much longer."

"I'm very sorry," Pam said. "My child was sick this morning. It won't happen again."

The nurse looked at Pam. "I've got my own problems," she said. "But I made it here on time."

RDCA Selection 2

RDCA Question Sheet             Student: _____
    Selection 2—Grade Level 2
                                Tester: _____

*Late for Work*                 Date: _____

A. Ask each question. Then circle a number to the right of the question to score the answer.

| Literal Recall Questions | Good | | Fair | | Poor |
|---|---|---|---|---|---|
| 1. Did Pam tell the truth or lie to the head nurse? | 5 | 4 | 3 | 2 | 1 |
| 2. List the things Pam did on her way to work. | 5 | 4 | 3 | 2 | 1 |

Interpretive Questions

| | | | | | |
|---|---|---|---|---|---|
| 3. Why did Pam lie to the head nurse about her reason for being late? | 5 | 4 | 3 | 2 | 1 |
| 4. How flexible do you think the head nurse should be when a worker comes in late? | 5 | 4 | 3 | 2 | 1 |

Active Questions

| | | | | | |
|---|---|---|---|---|---|
| 5. Was Pam right to lie to the head nurse about her reason for being late? Why or why not? | 5 | 4 | 3 | 2 | 1 |
| 6. What else would you have done? | 5 | 4 | 3 | 2 | 1 |

B. Add the circled numbers for each pair of questions to derive three combined scores.

C. Use this chart to find the rating for each combined score.

Literal Recall Score: _____

Interpretive Score:   _____

Active Score:         _____

> Good = 8 to 10 points
> Fair = 5 to 7 points
> Poor = 2 to 4 points

Literal Recall Rating: _____

Interpretive Rating:   _____

Active Rating:         _____

GO BACK if the literal recall and interpretive ratings are poor.
STOP HERE if the literal recall and interpretive ratings are fair.
CONTINUE if the literal recall and interpretive ratings are good.

# Teaching the School a Lesson

I was only thirteen years old, but I remember it as clearly as if it happened yesterday. Mrs. Taylor was the school counselor. She put me in the class with the smart kids because she had faith in me. She knew I wanted to straighten out.

I was so scared in that class! I read everything they said to read and wrote what they told me to write. And I tried to speak up in class, even though I wasn't very good at it.

Then one day, someone stole a teacher's car from the parking lot. I got blamed for it. I wasn't even at school that day. I was put on probation for a month and couldn't go to school.

I got behind in my classes real fast. The more I got behind, the more I lost interest in school. If they were going to treat me that way, I was going to teach them a lesson. I refused to learn from them. Soon they put me back into the class with the slower kids to show me who was boss.

Here I am today still trying to learn. I wonder what my life would have been like if things had been different. I guess we all wonder about things like that.

RDCA Selection 3

RDCA Question Sheet
   Selection 3—Grade Level 3

Student: _____

Tester: _____

*Teaching the School a Lesson*

Date: _____

A. Ask each question. Then circle a number to the right of the question to score the answer.

|  | Good | Fair | Poor |
|---|---|---|---|

**Literal Recall Questions**

1. Put these in the proper order:
He was blamed for stealing a car.
He got behind in his classes.
He was put in the class with the smart kids.     5  4  3  2  1

2. Why didn't the boy care that he was getting behind in his classes?     5  4  3  2  1

**Interpretive Questions**

3. Why do you think the boy got blamed for stealing the car?     5  4  3  2  1

4. What do you think his life might have been like if this hadn't happened?     5  4  3  2  1

**Active Questions**

5. Would you have put the boy into the class with the slower kids? Why or why not?     5  4  3  2  1

6. What would you have done if you were the boy who was put on probation?     5  4  3  2  1

B. Add the circled numbers for each pair of questions to derive three combined scores.

   Literal Recall Score: _____

   Interpretive Score:    _____

   Active Score:        _____

C. Use this chart to find the rating for each combined score.

> Good = 8 to 10 points
> Fair = 5 to 7 points
> Poor = 2 to 4 points

Literal Recall Rating: _____

Interpretive Rating:    _____

Active Rating:        _____

GO BACK if the literal recall and interpretive ratings are poor.
STOP HERE if the literal recall and interpretive ratings are fair.
CONTINUE if the literal recall and interpretive ratings are good.

# The Kids These Days

My grandfather can't say a good word about the kids these days. He read about a ten-year-old who mugged an older woman. He seemed almost glad because it proved his point. He also read that reading scores of high school kids have gone down lately. He says that kids don't care about getting an education. Kids, of course, only care about sex, drugs, and rock videos. He blames everything on kids these days.

My grandfather may be right, but he doesn't see how hard it is to grow up in today's world. There are a lot of drugs out there on the streets. My friends expect me to mouth off to our teachers. The violence in TV shows, rock videos, comics, and the news gives my friends plenty of ideas to think about.

Lots of my friends are angry people. They have little to look forward to in life. They know they have already lost the race to get ahead in this hi-tech world, so they have given up trying. They want to drag everyone else down with them. My grandfather doesn't know how much pressure there is on me.

RDCA Question Sheet     Student: _____
   Selection 4—Grade Level 4   Tester: _____

*The Kids These Days*      Date: _____

A. Ask each question. Then circle a number to the right of the question to score the answer.

| Literal Recall Questions | Good | | Fair | | Poor |
|---|---|---|---|---|---|
| 1. What does the grandfather think about the kids these days? | 5 | 4 | 3 | 2 | 1 |
| 2. Why is the grandchild angry with the grandfather? | 5 | 4 | 3 | 2 | 1 |

Interpretive Questions

| | | | | | |
|---|---|---|---|---|---|
| 3. What does it mean that some kids have "already lost the race to get ahead in this hi-tech world"? | 5 | 4 | 3 | 2 | 1 |
| 4. Do you think the grandchild's friends are basically "good kids" or "bad kids"? Why? | 5 | 4 | 3 | 2 | 1 |

Active Questions

| | | | | | |
|---|---|---|---|---|---|
| 5. Whose side are you on, the grandfather's or the grandchild's? Why? | 5 | 4 | 3 | 2 | 1 |
| 6. If you had a second chance, what would you change, if anything, about your school years? | 5 | 4 | 3 | 2 | 1 |

B. Add the circled numbers for each pair of questions to derive three combined scores.

C. Use this chart to find the rating for each combined score.

   Literal Recall Score: _____

   Interpretive Score:   _____

   Active Score:     _____

> Good = 8 to 10 points
> Fair = 5 to 7 points
> Poor = 2 to 4 points

Literal Recall Rating: _____

Interpretive Rating:   _____

Active Rating:     _____

GO BACK if the literal recall and interpretive ratings are poor.
STOP HERE if the literal recall and interpretive ratings are fair.
CONTINUE if the literal recall and interpretive ratings are good.

# Should I Build My Vocabulary?

My best friend at work uses lots of big words when she speaks. I don't even understand half the words that come out of her mouth. She says that we do our creative thinking with words. If we don't have a lot of precise and descriptive words to put into our thinking process, only general and vague thoughts will come out.

My friend says that successful people have big vocabularies. She remembers hearing about a study that was done on people who are at the top of their fields. They were given some kind of vocabulary test. No matter what field they were in, they all did extremely well on the test. The same test was then given to people at the bottom of their fields. I don't have to tell you the results of that study.

I want to build my vocabulary, but I'm simply too tired when I get home from work to concentrate. I barely even have the energy to watch television, let alone read. And, you know, I'm a little scared to start using bigger words. I would have to find new friends because my old friends wouldn't be able to understand me anymore.

RDCA Selection 5

RDCA Question Sheet
　　Selection 5—Grade Level 5

Student: _____

Tester: _____

*Should I Build My Vocabulary?*　　Date: _____

A. Ask each question. Then circle a number to the right of the question to score the answer.

| | Good | | Fair | | Poor |
|---|---|---|---|---|---|
| **Literal Recall Questions** | | | | | |
| 1. What kind of person is the author's friend at work? | 5 | 4 | 3 | 2 | 1 |
| 2. Describe the vocabulary study that was done and the results that were found. | 5 | 4 | 3 | 2 | 1 |
| **Interpretive Questions** | | | | | |
| 3. Tell what this quote means to you: "If we don't have a lot of precise and descriptive words to put into our thinking process, only general and vague thoughts will come out." | 5 | 4 | 3 | 2 | 1 |
| 4. If the author did build her vocabulary, do you think she would necessarily lose her friends? Why or why not? | 5 | 4 | 3 | 2 | 1 |
| **Active Questions** | | | | | |
| 5. Do you believe the study or do you think that the friend was making the whole thing up? Why? | 5 | 4 | 3 | 2 | 1 |
| 6. Would you want to build your own vocabulary? If so, do you have the time and energy it would take to do so? If not, why not? | 5 | 4 | 3 | 2 | 1 |

B. Add the circled numbers for each pair of questions to derive three combined scores.

　　Literal Recall Score: _____

　　Interpretive Score:　 _____

　　Active Score:　　　 _____

C. Use this chart to find the rating for each combined score.

| Good = 8 to 10 points |
|---|
| Fair = 5 to 7 points |
| Poor = 2 to 4 points |

Literal Recall Rating: _____

Interpretive Rating:　 _____

Active Rating:　　 _____

GO BACK if the literal recall and interpretive ratings are poor.
STOP HERE if the literal recall and interpretive ratings are fair.
CONTINUE if the literal recall and interpretive ratings are good.

# Can We Enjoy Our Work?

I read a book recently in which the author says we can earn a living by doing work we passionately enjoy.* It says that our fears of such things as failure, poverty, criticism, and aging hold us back. It also says that we hold ourselves back by stereotyping ourselves in rigid roles. Women continue to see themselves as providing for the emotional needs of others. At the same time, men continue to see themselves as providing for the physical needs of others. It says that we must begin to provide for our own needs by figuring out our strengths and weaknesses and the work we truly want to do. Then we must set goals for ourselves, find people whose leadership we can follow, research the market, and aggressively take control of our job search.

Well, I just don't believe that we all have the power to change our lives as much as the author suggests. Since we have responsibilities and obligations, we can't just take off in search of new identities. It's dangerous to pursue dreams that have little chance of turning into reality.

*From Nancy Anderson, *Work with Passion*, Carroll & Graff Publishers, Inc., New York, and Whatever Publishing, Inc., Mill Valley, Calif. (1984).

RDCA Selection 6

RDCA Question Sheet     Student: _____
  Selection 6—Grade Level 6  Tester: _____

*Can We Enjoy Our Work?*    Date: _____

A. Ask each question. Then circle a number to the right of the question to score the answer.

| Literal Recall Questions | Good | | Fair | | Poor |
|---|---|---|---|---|---|
| 1. What things supposedly hold us back from making a living by doing work we passionately enjoy? | 5 | 4 | 3 | 2 | 1 |
| 2. In what rigid roles do women and men keep themselves? | 5 | 4 | 3 | 2 | 1 |

Interpretive Questions

| | | | | | |
|---|---|---|---|---|---|
| 3. Why does the person who wrote this article disagree with the author of the book? | 5 | 4 | 3 | 2 | 1 |
| 4. Who do you agree with—the person who wrote the article or the author of the book? Why? | 5 | 4 | 3 | 2 | 1 |

Active Questions

| | | | | | |
|---|---|---|---|---|---|
| 5. If you went on a job search like the one described in the article, do you believe you would get the job you wanted? Why or why not? | 5 | 4 | 3 | 2 | 1 |
| 6. What do you enjoy doing? Could you earn a living by doing it? Why or why not? | 5 | 4 | 3 | 2 | 1 |

B. Add the circled numbers for each pair of questions to derive three combined scores.

  Literal Recall Score: _____

  Interpretive Score: _____

  Active Score: _____

C. Use this chart to find the rating for each combined score.

| |
|---|
| Good = 8 to 10 points |
| Fair = 5 to 7 points |
| Poor = 2 to 4 points |

Literal Recall Rating: _____

Interpretive Rating: _____

Active Rating: _____

GO BACK if the literal recall and interpretive ratings are poor.
STOP HERE if the literal recall and interpretive ratings are fair or good.

# PART 3

*Read to Learn,
Learn to Read*

# ☞ *Read to Learn, Learn to Read*

Part 3 of *Teach Someone to Read* is a manual of tutoring techniques. It develops a highly flexible method of tutoring based on the program's comprehension-based philosophy of how best to teach reading. That philosophy says that a person will most easily learn to read when the reading material is of interest to the person. In other words, a person learns to read when reading skills are taught within a meaningful context.

This part of the book applies the techniques of tutoring to a wide range of possible situations. Your task is to select the tutoring methods appropriate to use with a particular student. Before you start your sessions, read through all three chapters. Then, after you have tested the student and worked with him or her a few times, come back and review the materials that will help meet your specific tutoring needs.

Chapter 1 of this part is entitled "The Weekly Routine: Lesson Planning." It lays out a clear, easy-to-follow way to structure the individual sessions and provides two very thorough examples. Chapter 2 is entitled "Read to Learn: Comprehension." First, it gives you some background information on comprehension problems. Then it presents the theory and usage of reading topics, questioning strategies, comprehension training models, and activities that strengthen comprehension skills. Chapter 3 is entitled "Learn to Read: Word Recognition." It discusses the basic factors involved in word recognition: sight words, phonics, syllabication, language experience, vocabulary, and spelling. It also suggests a systematic way to teach intermediate writing skills.

Tutoring can be a highly rewarding personal experience. When a lesson goes well, you know it by the light in the student's eyes. The light tells you that he or she is building new connections. Few things are more satisfying than feeling that you are helping someone to make genuine changes in his or her life. So, good luck as you start out—but most of all, enjoy your tutoring.

# Chapter 1

# ☞ *The Weekly Routine: Lesson Planning*

*Becoming literate means
learning to read and write
words in order to learn and
share ideas.*

Lesson plans are the organizational core of your entire program. Certainly, you may have excellent rapport with a student, and you may have wonderful intentions. But if your tutoring sessions are poorly planned, they will lack focus and direction. If you have only a vague notion of where you want the student to go, how can you expect him or her to arrive there?

This chapter sets forth some guidelines for structuring lessons around student-centered content. It incorporates all the elements of good planning: content, creativity, continuity, and pacing. Your lessons should focus on content that is of particular interest to the student. They should show the student creative new ways to make qualitative leaps in understanding ideas and words. They should flow smoothly from activity to activity and from lesson to lesson. And they should be paced so that the student is gently pushed and never bored. Good lesson planning takes considerable time and effort, especially during the first month of tutoring. But you will quickly see that it has been time and effort well spent.

## Lesson Plan Format

The following lesson plan format presents a framework for organizing the activities you should include in a good two-hour session. If you find yourself tutoring for only an hour and a half, keep the same general format but reduce the length and number of activities.

1. Reading Topic

Select readings on a topic of interest to the student.

2. Questions

Use thorough questioning to help the student understand the information and ideas in the reading and to interpret them according to his or her own ideas, feelings, and values.

3. Comprehension Activities

Devise activities that help the student rearrange the ideas in the reading in order to achieve better comprehension and interpretation.

4. Word Recognition Activities

Prepare activities that pull out difficult words from the reading. Then use those words as the basis for further analysis and remedial work.

5. Vocabulary, Spelling, and Writing Activities

Construct activities that follow naturally from the reading to help the student develop each of these skills areas.

6. Evaluation and Suggestions for Next Session

After the session is over, write your evaluation of the lesson's activities and the student's difficulties and progress. Then make notes on ideas for the next session.

On page 51, you will find a sample (blank) lesson plan format to use as a model for your own lesson plan forms. The remainder of the chapter then develops sample first lesson plans for two hypothetical students. Sharon is a second-grade-level (beginning) reader, and Ross is a fourth-grade-level (intermediate) reader. An introductory case study for each student provides the basic information needed to analyze their reading problems. The case study is followed by a detailed explanation of the process for developing appropriate reading and remedial activities for the lesson. Then a specific lesson plan based on this information is presented.

Chapters 2 and 3 fill in the details of information and technique needed for planning later lessons. In both chapters, sequential lesson plans for Sharon and Ross continue to illustrate sample activities for each topic covered. After reading all three chapters in Part 3, you will be able to plan a complete and successful reading program for your student.

## SAMPLE LESSON PLAN FORMAT
### (Side One)

Student: _____    Lesson Number: _____

Level: _____    Date: _____

1. Reading Topic (_____ minutes)

2. Questions (_____ minutes)

3. Comprehension Activities (_____ minutes)

### (Side Two)

4. Word-Recognition Activities (_____ minutes)

5. Vocabulary, Spelling, and Writing Activities (_____ minutes)

6. Evaluation and Suggestions for Next Session

# Sample First Lesson Plan for Sharon, A Beginning Reader

*Case Study*

*Sharon is a 54-year-old woman who has difficulty reading one-syllable words. Although she attended school until the age of 16, she learned very little after her ninth birthday. At that time, she and her family were in a severe car accident. Having spent much of her childhood in and around hospitals, Sharon became interested in nursing. She has worked as a nurse's aide on and off for the past 25 years. She is the widowed mother of three teenagers.*

*Sharon was given the RDPA and was found to read basic four- and five-letter words inconsistently. Although she needs a good review of short vowels, vowel combinations such as* ea/ee *and* oo/ou *cause her the biggest problems.*

*Sharon was also given the level 2 selection of the RDCA. She did well on the interpretive and active questions. She had difficulty, however, with the literal recall items. In other words, Sharon can analyze the general idea of a reading, but she is unable to focus on its details.*

■   ■   ■

## In-Depth Lesson Planning

Now study the detailed explanation below. It is an annotated lesson plan for the first two-hour session with Sharon. It will explain how to use each section of the lesson plan format to develop appropriate reading and remedial activities. The activities are examples of those described in the corresponding activities sections in Chapters 2 and 3.

Student: _____*Sharon*_____  Lesson Number: _____*1*_____

Level: _____*2nd*_____  Date: _____*9/9*_____

1. Reading Topic (*30* minutes)

Sharon is interested in reading about health, disease, first aid, and nutrition. Since this is the first lesson, ask her to give you some background on her work as a nurse's aide. As she dictates the information to you, print her exact words clearly on a piece of lined paper. Don't leave anything out. Ask her leading questions whenever she stops talking. When you have half a page of printing, stop and help her read it back to you. This reading will go slowly. Since Sharon "wrote" the information, however, she will be able to read it. If necessary, read the text to her sentence by sentence and have her repeat each sentence after you.

This approach to reading is the "language-experience" approach. It is used mainly with people who can't read much of anything. Chapter 3 discusses language-experience stories in detail.

2. Questions (*20* minutes)

Now ask Sharon some questions about the story she dictated. Your questions could follow the questioning pattern developed in the RDCA, although you can skip literal recall questions since she just recalled her workday for you. A good analysis question would be this: Is there anything you do at work that could be done more efficiently? If so, how? A good generalization question would be this: Would you want the responsibilities of a nurse? Why or why not? For a reaction question you could ask this: Do you become emotionally involved with your patients? If so, with which ones? And for an action question you could ask this: How could you change your workday to make it better? Your goal is to use these prepared questions as a starting point for a discussion.

3. Comprehension Activities (*20* minutes)

An excellent activity to help Sharon understand what she reads would be to reorganize the narrative material into a chart, graph, or outline. In this case, for example, rework the language-experience story into a daily schedule of activities, with times and duties listed opposite each other. First, work together on setting up the chart for the schedule, with the times listed on the left and boxes in which to write the duties on the right. Then have Sharon dictate short phrases describing her duties. Insert the phrases in the appropriate boxes.

4. Word Recognition Activities (*20 minutes*)

Since Sharon needs a review of short words with short vowels, plan an exercise that uses the word *bed*, an important word in the lesson. *Bed* is part of the *ed* word family, and you can prepare a set of 3″ × 5″ word-family flash cards for drill work. On the first card, print *ed*. Go through the alphabet and find all the three-letter *ed* words and names: bed, fed, Jed, led, Ned, ped, red, Ted, wed. Prepare a separate card for each beginning consonant sound. Then go through the beginning blends listed on page 142 to find the ones that make common *ed* words: bled, fled, sled, sped, Fred. Prepare a separate flash card for each beginning blend sound.

Have Sharon read the first flash card that identifies the *ed* word family. Then add initial consonant sounds to form three-letter words for her to read. Go as fast as she is able. Take turns with her making up funny sentences using the words. For example: Jed was led to the red bed. Then work with the beginning blends. Show how adding a letter to the initial consonant sounds already used forms four-letter words: bed/bled, led/sled, fed/fled, ped/sped. Make up funny sentences using each pair of words. For example: He bled on the bed. She led with her sled.

5. Vocabulary, Spelling, and Writing Activities (*30 minutes*)

For a spelling activity, dictate to Sharon some of the *ed* words she just used. Give her the words she misspells to study as homework for a spelling quiz next session.

A good writing activity whenever a student dictates a language-experience story is to have him or her copy the story dictated. In this case, you could have Sharon copy either the original story or the schedule you made together.

6. Evaluation and Suggestions for Next Session

After the session is over, make a note of which activities went well and which ones fell flat. Write your observations of Sharon's abilities and disabilities. Note anything about her personal history that you learned, and whatever else you might want to remember. Then, while this lesson is still fresh in your mind, jot down any concrete ideas you have for the next or later lessons.

## The First Lesson Plan

The completed lesson plan that follows is based on the lesson-development process just explained.

Student: _____*Sharon*_____   Lesson Number: ____*1*____

Level: _____*2nd*_____   Date: _____*9/9*_____

1. Reading Topic (*30* minutes)

    *Sharon's duties as a nurse's aide: She will dictate a description, I'll write it, and she will read it back.*

2. Questions (*10* minutes)

    *Is there anything you do at work that could be done more efficiently? If so, how?*
    *Would you want the responsibilities of a nurse? Why or why not?*
    *Do you become emotionally involved with your patients? If so, with which ones?*
    *How could you change your workday to make it better?*

3. Comprehension Activities (*30* minutes)

    *We'll rework the language experience story together into a daily schedule in the form of a chart. List the times and duties opposite each other. Sharon will dictate short phrases describing her duties for me to write.*

| Time | Duty |
|------|------|
|      |      |
|      |      |
|      |      |
|      |      |

4. Word-Recognition Activities (*20* minutes)

*Review short e as in* **bed***. Use flash cards to drill the* **ed** *word family, three-letter words first: bed, fed, Jed, led, Ned, ped, red, Ted, wed. Make up funny sentences. For example: Jed was led to the red bed. Using additional flash cards, teach the beginning blends in bled, fled, sled, and sped, showing how to add a letter to a three-letter word to make a four-letter word: bed/bled, led/sled, fed/fled, ped/sped. Make up funny sentences using each pair of words. For example: He bled on the bed. She led with her sled.*

5. Vocabulary, Spelling, and Writing Activities (*30* minutes)

■ *Spelling: Sharon will spell* **ed** *words from the above exercise. Give her the misspelled words to study as homework for a spelling quiz next session.*

■ *Writing: Sharon will copy the language-experience story she dictated or the schedule we made together.*

6. Evaluations and Suggestions for Next Session

■ *Sharon knows a lot about nurse's aides and has strong opinions about nurses and doctors. She loves the patients.*

■ *She liked the chart; it was good repetition. Copying it took too much time.*

■ *The flash cards went easily. She does pretty well with simple short vowels.*

■ *Next time: Start drilling two-letter vowel combinations. Also, change the topic to heart attacks. Her sister recently had one and she wants to know more.*

# Sample First Lesson Plan
# for Ross, an Intermediate Reader

*Ross is an 18-year-old who dropped out of school a few years ago. He left after it was discovered that he could read only at the fourth-grade level. He spent his days in video arcades and his nights drinking with friends. Then he was arrested for stealing money from a neighborhood store to feed his video and alcohol habits. At this point, he realized that maybe he should learn to read so that he could change his life.*

*Ross took the RDPA and read the word lists fairly well. Although he stumbled over many of the multisyllabic words, he could read all but a few of the one-syllable words easily. From this assessment, it was determined that he read words at the fourth-grade level. Ross was also able to read the level 4 selection of the RDCA comfortably. He answered the straightforward literal recall questions with difficulty, but he did pretty well on the more abstract interpretive and active questions.*

■ ■ ■

## In-Depth Lesson Planning

Now study the detailed explanation that follows. It is an annotated lesson plan for the first two-hour session with Ross. It will explain how to address and develop each section of the lesson plan format. Remember, all the activities are examples of those described in Chapters 2 and 3.

Student: _____*Ross*_____ Lesson Number: ___*1*___

Level: _____*4th*_____ Date: _____*3/17*_____

1. Reading Topic (*30* minutes)

Ross's main interest is video games. You can find readings on the topic at your local library. The *Reader's Guide to Periodical Literature* lists video-game magazine articles in a number of categories. Computer magazines and books on video and computer games line library and bookstore shelves. For simpler readings that would be more appropriate for Ross to start with, check the children's section.

For this first lesson, use a one-page article from a children's magazine on how the bottom is falling out from under the video game market. Introduce the topic to Ross, and then have him read the article aloud to you. He will probably stumble over some of the more difficult multisyllabic words, which is all right. Help him read them, but note what they are for later analysis.

2. Questions (*10* minutes)

After Ross reads the article, discuss its contents with him. Good discussions rarely just happen on the spot. Questions to stimulate them must be planned ahead. The questioning strategy you plan should be patterned on the one developed for the assessment— literal recall, interpretive, and active questions.

For lesson planning purposes, prepare one question in each category to serve as lead questions. For the recall questions, you could ask Ross to give some facts from the reading or to reorganize the author's thoughts into his own words. For example: Why is the bottom falling out from under the video game market? For the interpretive question, encourage Ross to analyze the ideas presented in the reading or to make generalizations about them. For example: How do you think this will affect video arcades? For the active question, ask Ross what he feels about the situation or what he thinks should be done about it. For example: What would you do to change this downward trend?

Remember to use your questions as a way to stimulate discussion between the two of you. Since there is no such thing as a one-way discussion, you should give your opinions as well. Encourage Ross to ask you some questions, too.

3. Comprehension Activities (*20* minutes)

Activities that help comprehension are those that encourage a student to transform narrative material into another form. The form may be that of a chart, graph, diagram, list, outline, or picture. If Ross cannot take the author's words and make them his own in this way, he hasn't understood the article. In this case, have Ross make a bar graph depicting the rise and fall of the video game market as described in the article. Show him how to set up a bar graph with the dates of the years across the bottom and the number of potential machine sales (in thousands) on the left side. Then have him draw vertical bars for each year depicting the actual number of machines sold that year.

4. Word Recognition Activities (*20* minutes)

Since Ross had trouble with some two-syllable words in the RDPA test, review the major syllable rules during the first few sessions. The syllable rules are discussed in detail in Chapter 3.

Make a list of words in the article that follow the first syllable rule, the vowel-consonant/consonant-vowel (VC/CV) rule. The rule says that if there are two consonants between two vowels, divide between the consonants. For example, you might find and divide these words in the article: but/ton, mar/ket, suc/cess, ar/cade, fal/len, quar/ter.

After Ross reads the article, have him read the words you have divided. Next have him write and break them up himself. Ask him to try to come up with a rule about how to break up the words. Then teach him the VC/CV rule and have him tell how each word on the list follows the rule. Have him skim the text and underline other words that follow the VC/CV rule.

5. Vocabulary, Spelling, and Writing Activities (*40* minutes)

An excellent way to build vocabulary is to analyze prefixes and roots. Find a prefix or root that is used in the reading and generate more words from it. This activity is explained further in Chapter 3.

The video article might have the prefix *re-* used in such words as *rerun* and *repay.* Generate more words with *re-* as prefix. For example: react, recall, reheat, relearn. The dictionary can be a useful tool for this purpose. Explain that *re-* means again. Then have Ross define all the *re-* words you have selected.

For a good writing activity, have Ross write a paragraph telling if he agrees or disagrees with the article's gloomy outlook for video games. Go over the paragraph with him afterward. Correct only for spelling and one grammar point. Have him study the misspelled words at home to prepare for a short spelling quiz first thing next session.

6. Evaluation and Suggestions for Next Session

After the session is over, make a note of which activities worked well and which did not. Write down any observations you made about Ross's abilities and disabilities. Note any facts about his personal history that you learned, or anything else you might want to remember later. Then jot down ideas for future lessons while this lesson is still fresh in your mind.

## The First Lesson Plan

The following completed lesson plan is based on the lesson-development process just explained.

Student: _____ *Ross* _____    Lesson Number: ____ *1* ____

Level: _____ *4th* _____    Date: ____ *3/17* ____

1. Reading Topic (*30* minutes)

   *How the bottom is falling out from under the video game market. Ross will read a one-page article from a children's magazine aloud to me.*

2. Questions (*10* minutes)

   *Why is the bottom falling out from under the video game market? How do you think this will affect video arcades? What would you do to change this trend?*

3. Comprehension Activities (*20* minutes)

   *Ross will make a bar graph. It will depict the rise and fall of the video game market as described in the article.*

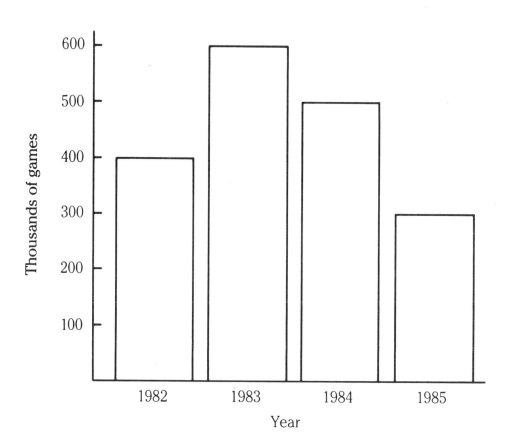

4. Word-Recognition Activities (*20* minutes)

*I'll list and divide VC/CV words from the article and have Ross read them. Then he'll write them on his own and break them up again. I'll have him try to come up with his own rule for dividing the words. I'll teach him the VC/CV rule and ask him to explain how each word on the list follows it. He will then skim the text, underlining other words that follow the rule.*

5. Vocabulary, Spelling, and Writing Activities (*40* minutes)

■ *Work with the prefix* **re-** *in words such as* **rerun** *and* **repay**. *Then look up more* **re-** *words in the dictionary, explain that* **re-** *means "again," and have Ross define all the words I selected.*

■ *Have Ross write a paragraph telling whether he agrees or disagrees with the article. Correct only for spelling and one grammar point. Have him study the misspelled words for a spelling quiz next session.*

6. Evaluation and Suggestions for Next Session

■ *Ross certainly does like video games. He read the article with little trouble.*

■ *The syllable and prefix exercises worked well.*

■ *He refused to write a paragraph and produced only one sentence.*

■ *Next time: Get Ross to write more. Also, go on to the next syllable rule.*

# Chapter 2

# ☞ *Read to Learn: Comprehension*

*Because we read in order to
learn, the words we read
must relate to topics we want
to learn about.*

This chapter discusses the concept of reading for meaning. It explores techniques for making reading interesting, enjoyable, and valuable to a student. The ability to decode words is basic to the reading process. There is, however, little reason to decode words except to understand their meaning in the context in which they were written.

Often, poor readers don't expect reading to make sense or to give them anything that is useful or fun. Their reading experiences have consisted primarily of reading words in phonically regular nonsense sentences; for example, Nan and Dan had a fan. Since it is much more difficult to read isolated, meaningless sentences than words in a meaningful context, it's easy to understand why poor readers become discouraged. It is important to integrate word recognition teaching methods with readings on topics that are interesting to a student. With this comprehension-based approach, you can help the student achieve his or her full reading potential.

## Selecting Reading Topics and Materials

### Case Study

*Beth was tutoring Doris, a very fashionable 34-year-old. Doris worked as a sales clerk in a large department store. Since her goal was to become a fashion buyer, Beth and Doris explored the world of fashion. They began by reading fashion magazines or written-down versions of articles from those magazines. It wasn't long, however, before they tired of these. So they expanded the topic to include such issues as why miniskirts, designer jeans, and other fashions had become fads; how clothing design reflects cultural aware- ness; how new fabrics are created by technology; and what forces determine the kinds of fashions that catch on. Beth found several good magazine articles on these topics that Doris could read with her help. Encouraged by her success, Doris was soon reading other articles on her own.*

■ ■ ■

Probably all of us have books at home that sit unread on our shelves. Although we were initially interested in them, we had to read only a few pages or a chapter to realize that they lacked appeal for us. A student reacts to reading material in the same way. As a tutor, it is part of your task to help the student find readable material that he or she finds relevant. The following suggestions will help you carry out this task.

- When you discuss reading topics, listen carefully to the stu- dent's tone of voice. Observe his or her body language. These will tell you a lot about the student's reaction to the various topics.

- If you are currently reading something with a student, ask for reactions to that material. Ask if there is anything your student finds particularly interesting or boring in it. This discussion might lead you to related topics that the student will also find interesting.

- Find out if the student has something at home that he or she would like to read but cannot because the words are too difficult.

- Ask if the student has a problem that might be solved more easily if he or she could do some reading on it.

- Find out if there is a subject the student has always wanted to explore but couldn't because of his or her inability to read.

Student: _____ *Sharon* _____   Lesson Number: _____ *2* _____

Level: _____ *2nd* _____   Date: _____ *9/16* _____

1. Reading Topic (*20* minutes)

   *Heart attack symptoms. I'll read the symptoms to Sharon from a medical book for lay people that I found at the library.*

2. Questions (*10* minutes)

   *I'll ask her to describe the symptoms, in detail, back to me. If she can't do that, I'll reread them to her. If she still can't describe them on her own, we'll discuss them together. Then I'll ask her why she thinks these symptoms indicate heart attacks.*

3. Comprehension Activities (*40* minutes)

   ■ *Sharon will dictate a language-experience story to me about her sister's heart attack. She told me about it last week. I'll ask her to describe which symptoms her sister had. She'll dictate the story, I'll write it, and then she'll read it back to me.*

   ■ *We'll make a simple listing of symptoms: chest pain, weak, tired, can't breathe, fluid in lungs, heart beats fast, tight chest, low blood pressure, fainting.*

4. Word-Recognition Activities (*20* minutes)

   ■ *Choose the words from the symptoms list with* **ea** *producing the long* **e** *sound: weak, breathe, beats. Sharon and I will brainstorm more* **eak** *words (beak, leak, peak, teak) and* **eat** *words (feat, heat, meat, neat, seat). I'll write them in two lists. Then I'll point to them one at a time and have Sharon say them quickly over and over.*

   ■ *Say, "I'm thinking of a word that rhymes with seat and it's something to eat. What is it?" Sharon guesses and takes a turn asking me to guess one of the words.*

5. Vocabulary, Spelling, and Writing Activities (*30 minutes*)

- *Give Sharon a spelling quiz of misspelled* **ed** *words from last week.*
- *Give her six* **eak** *and* **eat** *words to study for a spelling quiz next week.*
- *Sharon will copy the list of symptoms we made up earlier.*

6. Evaluation and Suggestions for Next Session

- *Sharon was very willing to talk about her sister's heart attack. She knew some symptoms but not others. It was a good exercise.*
- *She confused* **eak** *and* **eat** *a lot.*
- *Her copying took longer than I had expected.*
- *Next time: Work on* **ea** *words more. Get information on CPR (cardiopulmonary resuscitation); she feels she might need to use it to help her sister. Have her read something. The language-experience stories are too easy for her.*

Student: _____ *Ross* _____    Lesson Number: ___ *2* ___

Level: _____ *4th* _____    Date: _____ *3/24* _____

1. Reading Topic (*30* minutes)

*How much it costs to develop and market a computer game. I rewrote a newspaper article about the high costs and profits involved. I shortened the sentences and made it more readable for a fourth-grade-level reader.*

2. Questions (*20* minutes)

*How much do most video games cost to develop?*
*How much do they cost to market?*
*Describe the marketing process.*
*Are you surprised by the amount of money involved?*
*How would you get into the video game business?*
*Would you invest in video games if you had the money?*

3. Comprehension Activities (*20* minutes)

*Ross will make a pie graph showing how much each stage of developing and marketing a video game costs. All the information is in the article. Have him start with the idea stage and end with the marketing stage.*

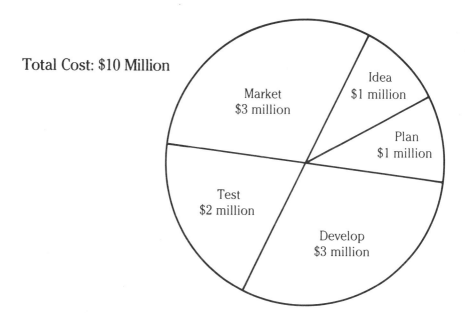

**Total Cost: $10 Million**

Idea $1 million
Market $3 million
Plan $1 million
Test $2 million
Develop $3 million

4. Word-Recognition Activities (*20 minutes*)

*Teach the second syllable rule: V/CV or VC/V. It says that if one consonant lies between two vowels, divide before consonant with first vowel long—divide after consonant with first vowel short. Have Ross work with the words from the article that follow either part of the rule, for example, pro/duce and re/vise for V/CV and prof/it and pan/ic for VC/V. Ask him to read the words and separate them, and then figure out the rule. To reinforce the activity, make a chart of other words that demonstrate both the V/CV and VC/V divisions and analyze it with Ross.*

5. Vocabulary, Spelling, and Writing Activities (*30 minutes*)

■ *For vocabulary building, have Ross find the word* **transition** *in the article and figure out its meaning. Brainstorm with him other* **trans-** *words; for example, transport, transfer, transit, transcontinental, transplant. Have him figure out that* **trans-** *means "across."*

■ *Ross will write the types of expenses involved in making and marketing a successful video game. I'll help him with spelling and punctuation. The point is to get him writing.*

6. Evaluation and Suggestions for Next Session

■ *Ross liked the article, but it was too easy for him to read. He understood the syllable rule; he knew it from his school days. He was able to write the types of expenses because most of the words he needed were in the article.*

■ *Next time: Find a harder article. Move on to three-syllable words. Give him a spelling quiz of words he misspelled when he wrote the types of expenses.*

## Suggested Topics

The following is a list of topics that generally interest adults and adolescents. If you and your student have difficulty choosing a reading topic, work through the list to find a few that have appeal. Then narrow the choices down to one.

READING TOPICS LIST

### Addictions

alcohol
drugs
cigarettes
food
work
self-help programs for addicts
personalities of addicts
biographies of addicts
alcoholic family structures

### Animals

pets
zoos
wild animals
circuses
evolution
biology
wildlife preservation
animal rights
experiments on animals

### Arts and Crafts

art and culture
art and religion
art history
specific crafts
how-to instructions for specific
     crafts
struggling artists

### Community Services

libraries
schools
driving instruction
police protection
clinics

### Crime

crimes against people
crimes against property
prisons
white- and blue-collar crimes
law enforcement
gun control
self-defense
personalities of criminals
antisocial behavior

### Emotions

joy
pain
anger
love
hate
sorrow

### Everyday Reading

telephone book
catalogs, price lists
menus
advertisements

newspapers/magazines/
   TV guides
warnings/warranties
labels/signs/posters/ads/
   containers
instructions and instruction
   manuals
bus and plane schedules
maps/charts/graphs
record jackets
contracts/leases
applications/forms
letters/junk mail
voter registration forms/ballots

## Food
cooking, baking
recipes
diets
natural foods
nutrition
food additives/chemicals
growing food
food stamps
food and religion
food and culture

## Health Care
diseases
medications
first aid/nursing/CPR
fitness/exercise/jogging/
   aerobics/yoga/weight lifting
medical discoveries/innovations
medical technology
costs of medical care
medical malpractice
Medicare/welfare

health maintenance
   organizations
mental health services
health insurance
family planning
right-to-life issues
right-to-die issues

## History
history of a country, a culture,
   an era, a religion, a city, a
   language, an ethnic group
immigration to the United States
social movements
prominent figures in history

## Injustices
social
political
racial
economic
religious
physical
equal rights
renters' rights

## Interpersonal Relations
family dynamics
sibling rivalry
effective problem solving
personal growth
emotional stability
therapy techniques
abusive relationships
assertiveness training
personality conflicts
loneliness

**Life Cycle**
childbirth
childhood
parenthood
raising children
aging
middle age
old age
death and dying

**Law and Government**
Constitution
citizenship
elections/voting
knowing your rights
small-claims courts

**Media**
current events
newspaper/TV/radio/
    magazines
movies/documentaries
advertisements
influence of the media on culture
influence of the media on politics
cable TV/rock videos/VCRs

**Money**
spending and saving
banking
credit
taxes and investments
income tax forms
budgeting
shopping for bargains
inflation
consumer education
IRAs
economic insecurity
buying a car

**Music**
classical, rock and roll, folk,
        jazz, gospel, country, blues,
        new wave, electronic
reading music
musicians and skills
performing artists/stars
musical instruments
dancing

**Psychic Phenomena**
astrology
ESP
tarot cards
witchcraft
voodoo
*I-Ching*
palmistry

**Reading for Pleasure**
novels (mystery, adventure,
        science fiction, romance)
short stories
plays
poetry
magazines
nonfiction (biography, autobio-
        graphy, adventure, how-to,
        science, history)

**Religion**
Bible/Bible stories
Scriptures/Psalms
comparative religions
spiritualism
Eastern religions
cults
meditation

## Science

plants and animals
space exploration
underwater exploration
scientific discoveries/innova-
    tions/experiments
astronomy
evolution
UFOs

## Sports and Recreation

sports current events
sports heroes/fans
team sports
individual sports
sports injuries/medicine
competition
camping/hiking/nature/back-
    packing
martial arts
self-improvement
games
gardening
travel
community recreation programs

## Technology

communications
computer technology
computers and education
inventions
transportation technology
technology and religion
people vs machines
electronics

## War

World War II
Vietnam War and its effects
the threat of nuclear war
"star wars"
soldiers and fighting
the effects of war on the
    economy
capitalism vs socialism

## Work

job-search skills/interviews/
    applications/want ads
occupational outlooks
technology and the job market
unions and the rights of workers
blue- and white-collar jobs
stress on the job
workers' needs for respect/
    fulfillment
job training programs
unemployment

## Youth

youth culture rebellion
peer pressure
sex/drugs/rock and roll
cars/motorcycles/racing
youth gangs
juvenile delinquency
superstars/fads
education/schools
family dynamics
cartoons/comics

Now practice selecting reading topics yourself before you meet with your student. Work through the activities in Practice Problem 2–1.

PRACTICE PROBLEM 2–1: Selecting Reading Topics

1. Read through the Reading Topics List on the preceding pages.

2. List the four topic categories that interest you most.

 

 

 

 

3. Write the topic categories in the order of your personal interest in reading about them.

   1st choice: _____

   2nd choice: _____

   3rd choice: _____

   4th choice: _____

4. Read through the subtopics listed in the category you picked as your first choice. List the three subtopics that interest you most.

 

 

 

5. Which of these subtopics would you like to read about first?

 

If you were being tutored, your tutor would begin by finding reading materials on this subtopic.

You will find a sample solution to this practice problem on pages 119–120.

# Finding Appropriate Reading Materials

Once you and your student have settled on a reading topic, you will have to find appropriate reading materials. Here are some suggestions for locating materials and for writing them down to grade level as necessary.

LIBRARIES

Many public libraries now have sizable "new reader" collections. These include both fiction and nonfiction books on topics of interest to adults and adolescents. The vocabulary and sentence structure in these books are simple, with reading levels ranging from the first to the fifth grade. Since the quality and variety of these books has been improving steadily, it is now possible to find appropriate reading materials for many literacy students. Call the main branch of your public library system to find out if it and/or other branches have a new reader collection. If not, ask if there are plans to add any and suggest that there is a real need for these types of books.

Libraries also have a number of resources for people seeking information about where to find materials. The subject card catalog is such a resource for fiction and nonfiction books. Magazine articles are listed in the *Reader's Guide to Periodical Literature* or in the computerized reader's guides that some libraries maintain. To find newspaper articles, check the library's selection of indexes to large-circulation newspapers such as *The New York Times*. Don't be shy about asking the librarians for help in using these resources.

Also explore the children's and young-adult sections of the library for books that might pass for adult-interest material. These sections of the library may have their own subject card catalogs and their own guides to periodical literature.

Now practice your own library skills by completing the exercise in Practice Problem 2-2.

PRACTICE PROBLEM 2–2: Using Your Library
List three library resources that will help you find information on the topic you decided most interested you in Practice Problem 2-1 on page 74.

1. _____

2. _____

3. _____

You will find a sample solution to this practice problem on page 120.

## PUBLISHERS
New reader books for adults and adolescents can be ordered directly from their publishers. A list of the major publishers of high-interest, easy-reading books can be found on pages 195–196. Send a postcard to each of them requesting a copy of its adult basic education catalog. By skimming through the catalogs, you will see the wide scope of materials available for literacy students. You will also find that most of the books are inexpensive.

## WRITING DOWN READING MATERIALS
Once you have found good material on a student's topic of interest, you may have to write it down to the student's reading level. This will be true especially for students who read below the fifth-grade level. Students who read at or above the fifth-grade level can read nearly anything you put in front of them with your help.

It's not difficult to write down reading materials. You shorten the sentences to a basic subject-predicate format, substitute short words for long ones, and leave out words and phrases that aren't critical to the meaning. You may also want to personalize the copy by adding examples that relate directly to the student's experience or to earlier discussions the two of you had. Just add sentences occasionally that interject ideas you have discussed. Use the student's name in the copy as often as possible.

The following will give you a concrete example of how to proceed. The original paragraph is taken from the level 6 reading selection of the RDCA on page 46.

**Original Paragraph**

I read a book recently in which the author says we can earn a living by doing work we enjoy. It says our fears of such things as poverty, peer pressure, and aging hold us back. It also says that we hold ourselves back by keeping ourselves in rigid roles.

**Written-Down Paragraph**

I just read a book. It says we can like the work we do. We are held back by our fears. We are afraid of being poor. We worry about what our friends think. We get scared of growing old. We see ourselves only in the old ways.

Some simple guidelines will help you assess the reading level of a written-down selection. The written-down paragraph above contains 48 words, 7 sentences, and 55 syllables. According to the chart below for selections of 100 words, the written-down paragraph is at the first-grade level. (Note that the number of sentences and syllables determined for each grade level in the chart overlap with those of the next grade level. This chart depicts only a rough approximation of readability.)

| *Readability Levels for 100 Words of Text* | | |
| --- | --- | --- |
| Grade Level | Number of Sentences | Number of Syllables |
| 1 | 12–20 | 105–115 |
| 2 | 10–15 | 115–125 |
| 3 | 8–11 | 120–130 |
| 4 | 7–9 | 125–135 |

Now practice writing down the paragraph in Practice Problem 2–3.

PRACTICE PROBLEM 2–3: Writing Down Material

Use the space below to write down the following paragraph to the third-grade level.

1. Rewrite the paragraph by shortening the sentences, substituting short words for long ones, and omitting unimportant words and phrases.
2. Mark off the first 100 words of your new paragraph.
3. Count the number of sentences.
4. Count the number of syllables.
5. Check the chart to see if your new paragraph is approximately at the third-grade level.
6. If necessary, adjust the length of sentences and words even more to bring the paragraph down to the third-grade level.

**Original Paragraph**

In the beginning, you may be intimidated by the thought of writing down a paragraph to a lower level. Perhaps you think there is a "correct" way of doing it. No, fortunately, there is no correct way. There is only a correct procedure. First, you must shorten the long sentences. Take out all the introductory clauses and write simple subject-predicate sentences. Next, you must substitute short words for long ones and omit unimportant words and descriptive phrases. Don't worry if the meanings of words change slightly. Sometimes such adjustments are unavoidable. The task, you see, is really not very complicated. Just do the best you can. You can practice by writing down this paragraph.

**Your Paragraph**

You will find a sample solution to this practice problem on page 121.

CREATING READING MATERIALS

You also may decide to create your own easy-reading materials if a student reads at the first- or second-grade level. Give your creativity free rein. You are not writing to be published, so don't worry if your sentences aren't absolutely perfect. Keep the words casual, personal, and simple. One page of double-spaced or printed material is plenty for any one lesson. You'll be doing more than just the reading during the session. For readability, just follow the guidelines in the chart on page 77.

# Expanding Topics

Suppose that after a student has read about a topic for a few sessions, the topic comes to a dead end. What do you do next? Remember, the reason the student chose that topic was to gain in-depth knowledge about something he or she considers interesting and worthwhile. So now is the time to explore related ideas and issues that will expand your coverage of the topic.

BRAINSTORMING

A simple brainstorming exercise is an excellent way to expand a topic. It's best to plan to brainstorm with someone else—preferably your student. But if he or she isn't interested, ask a friend or relative to brainstorm with you.

The brainstorming technique involves seeing how many ideas and issues related to the topic you and your partner can develop. To begin, write the topic at the top of a sheet of paper. Then, work with each of the following categories to generate as many related ideas and issues as you can.

- Historical/Political

- Economic/Material

- Psychological/Personal

- Social/Cultural

- Scientific/Technological

- Religious/Spiritual

Here is an example of a good brainstorming technique to use with a student whose topic is football. First, take what the student knows and use it. Have him or her tell you about the sport to see if this information suggests any related ideas and issues. Then, begin working your way through the list of categories. As the brainstorming progresses, make notes for each category, as shown in the example below.

TOPIC: FOOTBALL

**Historical/Political**

- the origins of football
- how the rules have evolved
- football legends and stories
- how teams end up in particular cities

**Economic/Material**

- the cost of tickets
- ticket scalping at the Superbowl and other big games
- professional players' salaries and contracts
- why football players promote various products
- the expenses required to maintain a professional football team
- the expenses required to maintain little league, high school, and college football teams

**Psychological/Personal**

- The emotions experienced by players when they are blocked or tackled and when they make errors
- how star players deal with their fans
- the personal sacrifices made by players training to be stars
- why fans get so worked up at football games
- the pressures under which game officials work
- the psychological tactics employed by coaches and key players to win games

## Social/Cultural

- why football is so popular in the United States
- attending a football game
- the social popularity of high school and college football stars

## Scientific/Technological

- how equipment has changed with technology
- why professional players can undergo various operations and still play
- the increasing role that sports medicine plays in football
- the effects of hormone and drug use on football players' performances
- how and why the playing turf has changed over the years
- the effect of technology, such as instant replay, on training techniques

## Religious/Spiritual

- the role that personal beliefs play in pain control
- pregame rituals for some players

Now use Practice Problem 2–4 to practice expanding a topic by brainstorming new ideas.

PRACTICE PROBLEM 2–4: Brainstorming
Take the topic that most interested you in Practice Problem 2–1 on page 74 and expand it as set forth in this section. Below is a chart to fill in using your topic.

Topic: _____

| Historical/Political | 1. |
| | 2. |
| | 3. |

| Economic/Material | 1. |
| | 2. |
| | 3. |

| Psychological/Personal | 1. |
| | 2. |
| | 3. |

| Social/Cultural | 1. |
| | 2. |
| | 3. |

| Scientific/Technological | 1. |
| | 2. |
| | 3. |

| Religious/Spiritual | 1. |
| | 2. |
| | 3. |

You will find a sample solution to this practice problem on page 122.

## ACTIVITIES FLOWCHARTS

With your student, select an item from your brainstorming list on which to focus first. You will use this to create a flowchart of activities designed to expand the student's knowledge and to improve his or her reading and comprehension skills.

A flowchart is a graphic device that is useful for planning activities. It shows how the activities flow from the source topic as natural and logical extensions or branches. A flowchart may be set up vertically or horizontally or in a circular fashion, as shown in the example on page 84.

This circular flowchart was made using the source topic from the football brainstorming list "attending a football game." It was written in the center of the flowchart so that the activities derived from it could be shown branching out from it in two layers. The first-layer activities are enclosed in circles. The second-layer activities, which flow from the first layer, are enclosed in boxes. You can see that there is enough material in this flowchart alone to last through a month of tutoring sessions.

Brainstorming and flowcharts are two excellent ways to expand a topic. These techniques help you find materials to engage your student in relevant reading. In turn, this leads to stimulating discussions, writing, and other skills development activities that sharpen the student's analytical abilities. Once a student has examined one item well, it's likely that he or she will apply these new analytical abilities in examining others.

Now use Practice Problem 2–5 to practice making a flowchart yourself.

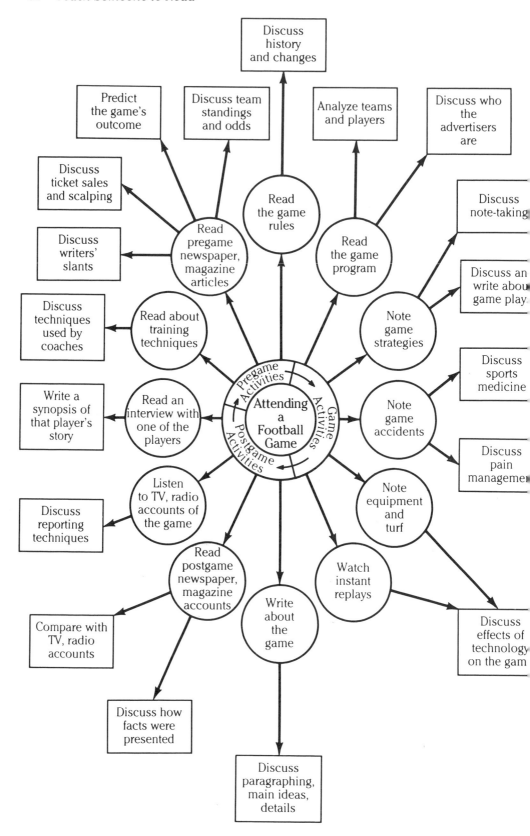

Discuss history and changes

Predict the game's outcome

Discuss team standings and odds

Analyze teams and players

Discuss who the advertisers are

Discuss ticket sales and scalping

Read the game rules

Discuss note-taking

Discuss writers' slants

Read pregame newspaper, magazine articles

Read the game program

Discuss techniques used by coaches

Read about training techniques

Note game strategies

Discuss and write about game play

Write a synopsis of that player's story

Read an interview with one of the players

Pregame Activities

Attending a Football Game

Game Activities

Postgame Activities

Note game accidents

Discuss sports medicine

Discuss pain management

Discuss reporting techniques

Listen to TV, radio accounts of the game

Note equipment and turf

Compare with TV, radio accounts

Read postgame newspaper, magazine accounts

Write about the game

Watch instant replays

Discuss effects of technology on the game

Discuss how facts were presented

Discuss paragraphing, main ideas, details

PRACTICE PROBLEM 2–5: Activities Flowchart
Fill in this simplified activities flowchart using an item from the topic
you brainstormed in Practice Problem 2–4, page 82.

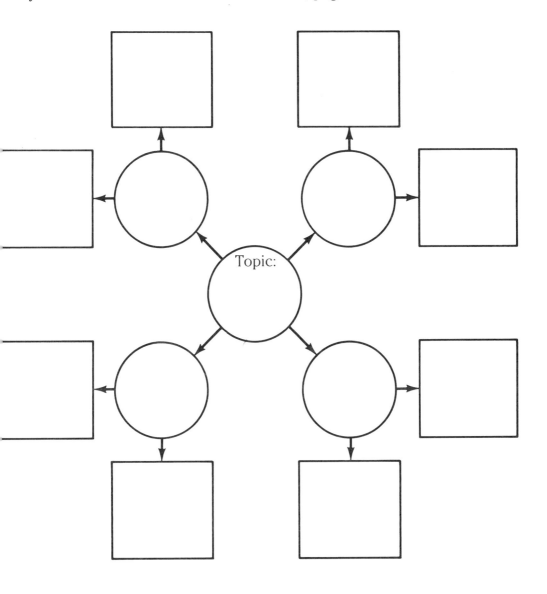

You will find a sample solution to this practice problem on
page 123.

---

*Checklist Review*

---

### Selecting Reading Topics and Materials

1. Decide on a topic with your student, either by selecting one of obvious interest to him or her or by using the Reading Topics List.

2. Find appropriate reading materials on that topic; or write down materials to the student's reading level; or create materials by writing your own stories.

3. Expand the reading topic when necessary by brainstorming and building activities flowcharts.

---

# Questioning for Comprehension

*Case Study*

*Jeffrey tutored Sonja, a 22-year-old mother of two. Sonja had trouble disciplining her children. She wanted to read about methods of child-rearing that were oriented toward strict discipline. Jeffrey found a number of good magazine articles and pamphlets for her.*

*Although Sonja could read the words, she had difficulty comprehending their meanings. So before each session, Jeffrey figured out how to focus the discussion on the current article and then prepared questions on each section of it. That helped Sonja analyze the article section by section. In this way, Jeffrey found that he could develop Sonja's ability to understand the author and draw out Sonja's ideas and opinions.*

■  ■  ■

So far, you have found your student's topic, expanded it, and selected and prepared appropriate materials. The next task facing you is developing questions to stimulate a discussion. The discussion will lead the student to a thorough comprehension of the reading.

Perhaps the most difficult—yet most important—role you have as a tutor is that of questioner. Asking good questions—ones that pull important concepts and insights from the student and lead to discussion—is crucial to the development of comprehension. The following techniques should help you develop that ability.

- Always have a focus for your questions. It is important to steer the discussion in a specific direction, even though you can't be sure where it will end up. Keep in mind one primary question to be answered before each session is over. Keep it in mind for directional purposes.
- Take your time. Don't fire off question after question, expecting immediate responses. Ask a question, wait for a response, and respond yourself before asking another question.
- Avoid asking narrow questions that have yes or no answers.
- Begin with concrete questions. Then progress to questions dealing with more abstract information and ideas.
- Keep your questioning open and nonjudgmental. Respect the student's responses, even when they differ from what your responses would be.
- Encourage the student to ask questions, too. He or she can learn how by following your technique, and the process can be exciting for both of you.
- Pay attention to pacing. A lively discussion is stimulating, but a long, drawn-out one with lengthy pauses is painful. Recognize when it is time to move your line of questioning into other areas. And most important, know when to end a discussion.

Student: _____ *Sharon* _____ Lesson Number: ____ *3* ____

Level: _____ *2nd* _____ Date: ____ *9/23* ____

1. Reading Topic (*30* minutes)

*Basic steps of CPR (cardiopulmonary resuscitation). Sharon wants to learn about CPR in case she needs to use it to help her sister. I'll teach her enough to give her courage to join a CPR training workshop. I called the Red Cross and got a CPR booklet written at the fourth-grade level. It's a little too hard for Sharon, but I'll help her read it.*

2. Questions (*10* minutes)

*How do you open the airway?*
*How do you restore breathing?*
*How do you get the blood circulating again?*
*Do you think you can learn to do it? Why or why not?*
*Do you think you could actually use it on your sister? How?*

3. Comprehension Activities (*20* minutes)

■ *Work with Sharon to make a wall chart of the three basic CPR steps: A = Airway, B = Breathing, and C = Circulation. Under each step, add a description of how you do it, as dictated to me by Sharon.*
■ *If Sharon decides she wants to join a course, call the Red Cross together to find out when and where the courses are given.*

4. Word-Recognition Activities (*20* minutes)

■ *Since the basic CPR steps are in alphabetical order (A, B, C), we will do some alphabetizing. I'll have Sharon write the alphabet and sound out the letters.*
■ *I'll have her pick ten words from the reading, write them on 3" × 5" cards, and then put the cards in alphabetical order. I'll help her as needed.*

5. Vocabulary, Spelling, and Writing Activities (*40* minutes)

■ *Sharon will dictate a language-experience story to me about what she would do if she found her sister passed out on the sofa. I'll write the story as she dictates. Then she will read it and copy it for her writing activity.*

■ *I'll give her a spelling quiz of the* eak *and* eat *words she studied last week.*

6. Evaluation and Suggestions for Next Session

■ *The Red Cross booklet was too difficult for Sharon, but she wanted to read it because she was interested. For next week, I'll write the material down to her level.*

■ *She doesn't know the whole alphabet, so I assigned it to her for homework.*

■ *Next time: Read written-down CPR booklet. Review alphabet.*

Student: _____ *Ross* _____    Lesson Number: _____ *3* _____

Level: _____ *4th* _____    Date: _____ *3/31* _____

1. Reading Topic (*30* minutes)

   *Arcade video games vs home video games. I'll have Ross read aloud a magazine article from a recent copy of a children's computer magazine. I'll keep notes of the words he stumbles over.*

2. Questions (*15* minutes)

   *How does the article describe the two types of games?*
   *Does the author think home video games can be as exciting as arcade video games?*
   *How does the difference in development costs affect the two markets?*
   *How would you improve the home video game market?*
   *Would you like to develop video games? How would you go about it?*

3. Comprehension Activities (*20* minutes)

   *Ross will make a chart comparing and contrasting arcade video games to home video games. First he will fill in information from the article. Then he'll add the things he knows from his own experience.*

| Arcade Games | Home Games |
|---|---|
|  |  |
|  |  |
|  |  |

4. Word-Recognition Activities (*15 minutes*)

■ *Review the words Ross stumbled over in the reading. Then we'll review the two syllable rules by finding the words that follow the rules.*

■ *Next, Ross will find the words ending in* -tion *in the reading and break them into syllables, emphasizing the suffix. For example, pro/duc/tion, in/tro/duc/tion, tran/si/tion. He will then brainstorm more* -tion *words and use them in sentences.*

5. Vocabulary, Spelling, and Writing Activities (*40 minutes*)

■ *Give Ross a spelling quiz of the words he misspelled last week in the sequence writing activity.*

■ *For vocabulary development, work with the hard words in the reading. Have Ross break them up, pronounce them, and figure out what they mean from context clues.*

■ *Ross will write a paragraph about his favorite video game, telling why he likes it best. If he has trouble writing the paragraph, he'll speak it into my tape recorder. Then I'll play it back and he will try to write it. I'll correct for spelling and for periods also, as he seems to write in run-on sentences.*

6. Evaluation and Suggestions for Next Session

■ *The article was a little too hard for Ross to read, but with my help it worked out. He certainly has a favorite game, and the tape recorder technique worked well. He likes learning new words.*

■ *Next time: Work with run-on sentences and give a spelling quiz of missed words. Find a simple grammar book for reference in sentence writing.*

## A Questioning Pattern

Having a pattern for your questions will help you avoid insulting or confusing a student with questions that are too simple or too abstract. The RDCA questioning pattern (pages 32–33) will let you ask thought-provoking questions while progressing from the concrete to the abstract. Here is a full description of that pattern. As you read it through, look back at the RDCA Question Sheets (pages 36–46) to see how they follow the pattern.

LITERAL RECALL QUESTIONS

1. **Describe:** observe, recall, state details, recognize facts

   Ask the student to describe information stated explicitly in the reading. As you draw this information out, focus the student on adhering to what the author has said.

   Types of Questions:
   Recall the facts.
   State the details of what happened.
   What came first, second, third?
   List the words that described . . .

2. **Reorganize:** translate, paraphrase, summarize, classify, categorize, recognize main ideas

   Ask the student to reorganize the information and ideas stated explicitly in the reading into his or her own words. This will make it easier for the student to grasp the meanings of words.

   Types of Questions:
   Restate the information and ideas using your own words.
   What was the main point made by the author?
   Categorize the author's ideas.
   Classify the information.
   Summarize the information and ideas using your own words.
   List the important facts and ideas to remember.
   What does the author think about . . . ?

INTERPRETIVE QUESTIONS

**3. Analyze:** interpret, infer, synthesize, compare, contrast

Ask the student to analyze ideas that go beyond those stated explicitly in the reading. You want the student to extract deeper meaning from the words by "reading between the lines."

Types of Questions:
What does it mean that . . . ?
Compare and contrast . . .
What motivates the character(s)?
Why did certain events happen?
What do you think about the facts that were presented?

**4. Generalize:** evaluate, judge, conclude, conceptualize, form opinions, take a stand

Ask the student to take the information and ideas already described and analyzed and to generalize to larger, broader issues. You want the student to take information written by someone else and use it to create his or her own conceptual understandings.

Types of Questions:
Should it have happened the way it did?
What do you think about the situation or the character(s)?
If something were changed, how would the change affect the outcome?
Do you agree with the author? Why or why not?
What is your opinion?
What conclusions can you draw?

ACTIVE QUESTIONS

**5. React:** respond, react emotionally, make value judgments, appreciate

Ask the student to react personally or emotionally to the feelings brought up in the reading. The student should tell you what he or she *feels* about the subject rather than what he or she *thinks* about it.

Types of Questions:

What advice would you give . . . ?

Was it morally right?

Would you have done the same thing?

What is your personal emotional reaction to the story situation?

**6. Act:** change, do

Ask the student to decide how he or she could act upon the thoughts and feelings brought up in the reading. You are seeking an active response in addition to the more passive, intellectual ones asked for earlier. You are encouraging the student to look at actions and consequences that could occur beyond the tutorial sessions.

Types of Questions:

What could you do about it?

How could you change this situation?

What alternatives are there?

Can you apply the reading to your own life situation?

Now practice reading a short-story excerpt and developing questions for it in Practice Problem 2–6.

PRACTICE PROBLEM 2–6: Questioning Pattern

Read the following excerpt from a short story on nurse's aides*
written at the third-grade level. Then write one sample for each type
of question.

> Jean got up and turned off the TV. Then she went back to
> the sofa. Cindy, her friend, was sitting there. Cindy's face looked
> sad. But Jean had a big smile on her face.
>
> "Don't you just love movies about hospitals?" Jean asked.
> "Life, death, health, sickness—so much goes on. It's all so
> important. It's never boring. I want to work in a hospital."
>
> "That's just a TV show," Cindy said. "It's just a movie. It's
> not like that in a real hospital. All you saw were the pretty things.
> The drama. You didn't see all the ugly things. The bed-wetting.
> The people who can't feed themselves. The ones who yell at
> you."
>
> Cindy hated hospitals. She knew what they were like.
> Watching people die wasn't pretty.

*From *Drama at the Hospital* (Career Reader No. 1—Nurse's Aide) by Nadine Rosenthal. David S.
Lake Publishers, Belmont, Calif. (1986).

## Literal Recall Questions

1. Describe: _____

2. Reorganize: _____

## Interpretive Questions

3. Analyze: _____

_____

4. Generalize: _____

_____

## Active Questions

5. React: _____

6. Act: _____

_____

You will find a sample solution to this practice problem on page 124.

---

*Checklist Review*

---

Questioning Pattern

Literal Recall Questions
*Describe* = Describe the content of the reading.
*Reorganize* = Reorganize the reading into your own words.

Interpretive Questions
*Analyze* = Analyze the ideas from the reading.
*Generalize* = to larger issues.

Active Questions
*React* = React emotionally to the reading.
*Act*  = Act on your thoughts and feelings about the reading.

---

# Activities for Comprehension

*Case Study*

*Rose had been tutoring Victor regularly for five months. Victor could read almost every word Rose put in front of him, but he comprehended almost nothing. No matter how many questions Rose asked about the reading material, Victor couldn't focus on the content. Rose then decided to try another technique. Instead of asking so many questions, she decided to reorganize the key facts and ideas from narrative form into lists, charts, and other forms. From then on, after Victor had read a story, they worked together to develop a sequence of events, a list of characters, a chart depicting pros and cons, or some other form of reorganization. This manipulation of the words was just what Victor needed. He was then able to reorganize any reading so that he could comprehend it.*

■   ■   ■

Recent brain reseach has shown that we do not learn in logical sequences. Rather, we learn by detecting patterns in what we see, hear, and read. Then we automatically create categories in our brains to organize the incoming patterns for later recall.

Most readers have well-developed mental systems for seeing and organizing patterns—for learning. People who have been nonreaders or low-level readers all their lives, however, are unlikely to have such developed mental systems. As a result, it is often harder for them to learn. That is why it's important to ask a student the kinds of questions that will help develop the conceptual and organizational skills in which he or she is weak. Then you can choose comprehension activities that will help strengthen the student's ability to detect patterns and form categories while reading.

The following comprehension activities are organized in the same way as the comprehension questions. Note that a comprehension activity followed by an asterisk may serve also as a writing activity. Additional suggestions for writing activities can be found in Chapter 3.

Student: _____*Sharon*_____ Lesson Number: ___4___

Level: _____*2nd*_____ Date: ___*9/30*___

1. Reading Topic (*30 minutes*)

    *CPR (continued): I've simplified the Red Cross CPR booklet so Sharon can read it more easily. It presents a short, simple sequence for the eight steps.*

2. Questions (*10 minutes*)

    *What do you do first, second, third?*
    *What do you look, listen, and feel for? How do you do this?*
    *Why do you tilt the head back and hold the jaw up?*
    *How do you pump the lungs?*
    *Which step is most difficult for you?*
    *How would you get help from other family members?*

3. Comprehension Activities (*40 minutes*)

    ■ *On a second copy of the CPR reading, I have erased every tenth word and put those words into a list. Sharon will fill in the blanks using the word list. (This is the cloze procedure.)*
    ■ *She will tell me the eight CPR steps, and I'll write each one on a 3" × 5" card. She will read the cards aloud and put them into chronological order.*

4. Word Recognition Activities (*20 minutes*)

    ■ *The reading says to look, listen, and* **feel** *for breathing. We'll use* **feel** *to brainstorm* **ee** *words of all types. Then, as a review of last week's session, we'll brainstorm* **ea** *words of all types. Teach the rule: When two vowels go walking, the first one does the talking.*
    ■ *Sharon will put the* **ee** *and* **ea** *words on 3" × 5" cards and alphabetize each group by first letter and then by end letter.*
    ■ *As a final step, I'll ask her to write the alphabet, which she studied as last week's homework.*

5. Vocabulary, Spelling, and Writing Activities (*20 minutes*)

  ■ *We'll make up sentences using words we brainstormed above. Then I'll dictate the sentences to her. She will write them, and then she'll correct them herself.*
  ■ *She will choose five of the words to learn to spell for next week.*

6. Evaluation and Suggestions for Next Session

  ■ *My rewritten version of the eight steps worked much better than the original used last week. The cloze procedure took longer than expected, but it was a very good exercise.*
  ■ *Sharon is starting to get the* ee *and* ea *words now.*
  ■ *Next time: Move on to other vowel combinations. Start work with health and nutrition. Sharon requested it because she doesn't want to have a heart attack. She feels she eats too much red meat and gets too much cholesterol.*

Student: _____ *Ross* _____    Lesson Number: ____*4*____

Level: _____ *4th* _____    Date: _____*4/7*_____

1. Reading Topic (*30* minutes)

   *Psychological aspects of playing video games. Ross will read a magazine article that says the games are addictive because they are totally involving and provide an escape from everyday troubles. As he reads each paragraph, I'll stop him and ask if he understood it. If he didn't, he will determine if the cause was difficulty with a word, a sentence, or the whole thing. We'll clarify before continuing.*

2. Questions (*20* minutes)

   *Give the author's five reasons for saying that video games are addictive.*
   *Reorganize the reasons so the one that is most important to you comes first.*
   *Can you add more reasons of your own?*
   *Do you agree that the games are addictive? Why or why not?*
   *Does the author mean that video games are bad because they are addictive to some people? Discuss.*
   *Do you think there should be a Video Game Players Anonymous on the order of Alcoholics Anonymous? Why or why not?*

3. Comprehension Activities (*20* minutes)

   *Focus on the ways video game addiction is like and unlike addiction to alcohol and drugs. Ross will make a chart of the information in the article and from his own experience.*

| *Like Alcohol and Drugs* | *Unlike Alcohol and Drugs* |
|---|---|
|  |  |
|  |  |
|  |  |

4. Word-Recognition Activities (*20 minutes*)

■ *Review the words Ross stumbled over. If any of them follow the two syllable rules learned previously, review the rules.*
■ *Take words ending in* -ly *from the reading, break them into syllables, and then concentrate on the suffix. Discuss how* -ly *at the end of a word is pronounced as* lee.

5. Vocabulary, Spelling, and Writing Activities (*30 minutes*)

■ *Give a spelling quiz of misspelled words from last week.*
■ *Take the root* press, *as in* impressive, *and build more* press *words; for example, depress, repress, oppress. Explain that in these words,* press *means to "press down."*
■ *I typed Ross's writing from last week, leaving out all punctuation. We'll discuss sentences as expressions of complete thoughts and put periods where they belong.*

6. Evaluation and Suggestions for Next Session

■ *Ross talked a lot about being addicted to video games. He is now getting over it. He likes filling in the charts. The sentence activity was helpful and he's beginning to get the idea.*
■ *Next time: Continue with sentence structure. We might start reading about educational computer games.*

## Literal Recall Activities

ACTIVITIES TO HELP YOUR STUDENT DESCRIBE

These activities will help a student describe by requiring him or her to find and list details that are explicitly stated in the reading.

- Ask the student to list all the events that took place in the reading.*

- Have the student write descriptions of two or three major things that happened in the reading.*

- Have the student locate names, dates, and other similar details in the reading.

- Ask the student to find on a map any geographical locations mentioned in the reading.

- Remove every tenth word from the reading and make a list of them. Then ask the student to read the selection aloud and replace the words correctly.*

- Choose a word or phrase in the reading and have the student find and underline it.

- Select a detail in a paragraph of the reading and have the student read the paragraph and identify the detail.

- Select a paragraph in the reading that proves a point. Then ask the student to skim through the reading to find the paragraph.

- Make a list of factual questions about the reading that must be answered by filling in omitted words. Then have the student fill in the words.*

- Ask the student to list five words that describe a character, a setting, or some other feature of the reading. Then have the student write a description of that feature in his or her own words.*

- Have the student look up the dictionary meanings of unfamiliar words in the reading and use those words in sentences. He or she may then write the sentences.*

- Have the student look up synonyms of unfamiliar words in the reading and use those words in sentences. He or she may then write the sentences.*

*This may also serve as a writing activity.

- Take turns asking and answering each other's recall questions about the reading. Look up any answers you don't know.
- Go through the reading with the student, underlining items that will be important to remember.
- Discuss the sequence of events in the reading—what happened first, second, third, and so forth.
- Determine with the student which situations and events led to other things happening in the reading.
- Prepare a partial outline of the sequence of events in the reading. Then have the student complete it.*

ACTIVITIES TO HELP YOUR STUDENT REORGANIZE

These activities will help your student reorganize information and ideas in the reading. They require him or her to restate, sort out, chart, map, diagram, sketch, picture, or manipulate details and concepts that are either stated or implied.

- Write each event, person's name, and idea in the reading on a flash card and shuffle the cards. Then have the student sort the cards into three categories.
- Break up a sentence from the reading into words or phrases, write each one on a flash card or slip of paper, and shuffle them all. Then have the student reposition the words and phrases in the correct sequence.
- Discuss figurative language in the reading, such as metaphors and similes.
- Help the student make a chart comparing and contrasting concepts in the reading.*
- Help the student make a chart showing the pros and cons of ideas in the reading.*
- Prepare a list of phrases that describe the content of the reading. Then have the student choose the one(s) he or she thinks relate most precisely.
- Analyze the construction of sentences in the reading. Show the student how descriptive phrases add to the meaning of the basic sentences.

*This may also serve as a writing activity.

- Have the student make a list of important facts to remember from the reading and rank them in order of importance.*
- Ask the student to make a picture, chart, map, diagram, or flowchart depicting or clarifying the story, a scene, or a group of facts in the reading.*
- Reproduce several paragraphs in the reading on separate cards or pieces of paper, and then write a title for each one on another set of cards or paper. Ask the student to match the titles with the paragraphs.
- If the reading can be reorganized to make better sense, ask the student to do that.
- Have the student make a list of words that describe or relate to the reading and use them in sentences.*
- Have the student describe his or her mental picture of a character, setting, or other element in the reading.
- If the reading suggests any experiments within the student's capability, have him or her perform them.
- If the reading gives amounts for distances, costs, or quantities, have the student think up simple math problems that use the data.

These activities will also help a student reorganize information and ideas in the reading. They have him or her locate, summarize, and outline main ideas, make up titles, and define problems.

- Have the student locate the sentence in a paragraph that contains its main idea. Then ask him or her to compare that sentence to others in the paragraph to see how they contribute related information.
- Ask the student to suggest an original title for the reading and/or for each paragraph.
- Have the student write one word or phrase to describe a paragraph in the reading.*
- Have the student write one paragraph that summarizes the main points in the reading.*

*This may also serve as a writing activity.

- Have the student prepare a written outline of the main ideas in the reading.*
- Make up a variety of sentences about the main idea of the reading. Then have the student select the one he or she thinks is best and tell you why.
- If a problem is presented in the reading, ask the student to define it.

## Interpretive Activities

ACTIVITIES TO HELP YOUR STUDENT ANALYZE
These activities will help your student analyze information and ideas in the reading. They encourage the student to give personal meaning to printed material.

- Have the student make a chart comparing or contrasting the author's point of view to his or her own thoughts on the reading's subject.
- Copy a sentence from the reading that implies something other than the obvious. Then have the student reread it to find the implied meaning.
- Have the student identify two possible meanings for an ambiguous statement in the reading.
- Ask the student what the author probably meant by a particular statement.
- Ask the student how he or she would explain the meaning of the reading to a young person.
- Ask the student to read a paragraph and then tell him or her what you think it means. You may tell the truth or lie. The student may agree or disagree with you but must give reasons.
- After the student has finished a reading, ask, "Does it mean that . . . ?" The student must answer yes or no and give an explanation.
- After the student has finished a reading, ask if he or she would have written it another way. If so, how?

*This may also serve as a writing activity.

- Have your student read a short article sentence by sentence. After each sentence, ask, "What does it mean to you?"

- Have the student stop reading when he or she comes to an unfamiliar word. Discuss the meaning of the word and how it contributes to the meaning of the sentence.

- Help the student understand sentence construction. Identify the core parts of a sentence (subject and main verb). Then identify the descriptive parts (introductory phrases, prepositional phrases, adjectives, and adverbs). Show how the descriptive parts affect the meaning of the sentence.

- Ask the student to estimate the probability that an event in the reading might actually happen.

- Have the student analyze ways in which the author manipulated facts in order to emphasize his or her point of view.

- Discuss the validity of an argument put forth by the author.

- Compare or contrast each other's personal opinions about the reading.

- Have the student evaluate the tone (humorous, technical, sarcastic, serious, and so forth) of the reading and identify the parts that led to this evaluation.

## ACTIVITIES TO HELP YOUR STUDENT GENERALIZE

These activities will help your student make generalizations about the reading. They encourage him or her to evaluate, form opinions, and make judgments regarding the reading's content.

- Have the student make a chart showing the differences between the author's point of view, his or her own point of view, and your point of view.*

- Have the student list the reasons why the reading is relevant or irrelevant to his or her own life.*

- Ask the student to draw as many conclusions as possible from the reading and to list them.*

- Have the student first list factual events in the reading and then fictional events.*

*This may also serve as a writing activity.

- Interrupt the reading occasionally to ask the student to predict what might come next.
- Ask the student to identify opinions that were presented as facts in the reading.
- Ask the student to identify rash generalizations made in the reading.
- Ask the student for an opinion on whether the facts used by the author are correct.
- Have the student list a variety of outcomes that might result from events in the reading. Then select the outcomes that each of you likes best.*
- Ask the student to identify the evidence that led to certain conclusions presented in the reading.
- Select three statements from the reading and ask the student to evaluate them for accuracy.

## Active Activities

ACTIVITIES TO HELP YOUR STUDENT REACT

These activities will encourage your student to react to the reading on a personal, emotional level. This allows him or her to voice the feelings behind the thinking involved in the preceding activities.

- If the reading presents an issue, have the student select a position on it and tell why he or she takes that position.
- Ask the student to compare his or her own personal values to those expressed by the author. Then have the student make a chart listing the author's opinions that he or she thinks are right and those he or she thinks are wrong.*
- Have the student list the reasons why he or she does or does not identify with the characters or ideas in the reading.*
- Ask the student to identify emotionally loaded phrases used by the author to sway the reader. Then ask for reactions to those phrases.
- Ask the student to analyze issues that were not explicitly stated in the reading, that is, to "read between the lines."

*This may also serve as a writing activity.

## ACTIVITIES TO HELP YOUR STUDENT ACT

These activities will encourage your student to participate in changing some of the things in the reading about which he or she feels strongly.

- Ask the student to identify and list the things mentioned in the reading that he or she would like to change.*
- Ask the student to rewrite the reading according to his or her own point of view.*
- Go to the library with the student to look for more information on the topic of the reading.
- Have the student prepare a set of interview questions and interview a person who is knowledgeable on the topic.*
- Ask the student to write to organizations, congressional members, and other sources for more information on the topic.*
- Work with the student to develop a strategy for improving or ending a situation in the reading.
- Have the student write a critical review of the reading.*
- Ask the student to list ways in which the information in the reading can be used by others he or she knows.*
- Have your student read more about the causes of the conditions or events in the reading.

## ORAL FLUENCY ACTIVITIES

These activities will help your student develop good oral reading skills, which are often a real problem for literacy students. Begin with easy readings and progress to more difficult ones at a pace that is comfortable for the student. Remember not to inhibit your student by overcorrecting.

- Try duet reading. Have the student follow along as you point to the words and read them aloud. Then ask him or her to read aloud with you.
- Engage in some echo reading. Read a phrase aloud and then have the student read the same phrase aloud again. Continue alternating in this fashion.

*This may also serve as a writing activity.

- Have the student read phrases rather than words. For example, instead of having the student read *I / went / to / the / store / for / some / milk./*, ask him or her to read *I went / to the store / for some milk.*

- Make up a list of prepositional phrases and put each one on a flash card. Then have the student read each phrase as a unit; for example, in her hand, across the table, from the bank.

- Ask the student to reread a paragraph he or she just read aloud, using more expression this time.

- Encourage the student to make informed guesses about unfamiliar words. If a guess is incorrect but still makes sense, the student is at least showing that he or she can predict the words that will come next, an important comprehension skill. Do not, however, encourage wild guessing.

- Repeat incorrectly read phrases or sentences exactly as read so the student can hear what he or she just said.

- Tape the student's oral reading and play it back during the session.

Now use Practice Problem 2–7 to practice planning comprehension activities to enhance a reading.

PRACTICE PROBLEM 2-7: Comprehension Activities
Reread the short story excerpt about hospitals in Practice Problem 2-6 on page 95. Then, from each set of comprehension activities, choose one activity that would help someone comprehend the excerpt. Adapt the activities to the excerpt and write them in the spaces below.

### Literal Recall Activities

Describe: _____

_____

_____

Reorganize: _____

_____

### Interpretive Activities

Analyze: _____

_____

_____

Generalize: _____

_____

_____

### Active Activities

React: _____

_____

Act: _____

_____

### Oral Fluency Activity

_____

_____

_____

You will find a sample solution to this practice problem on page 125.

# Comprehension Training Models

*Case Study*

*After working on comprehension development with Lynn for six months, Ruth saw little progress. Hadn't she done everything right? She had taken time to develop her questioning technique and had given Lynn lots of activities. Yet nothing seemed to make an impact. Lynn still couldn't comprehend what she read, no matter how easy the material.*

*Another tutor helped Ruth with her dilemma. He had read that poor readers need to be taught how to ask their own questions in order to increase their comprehension ability. He told Ruth that poor readers must be shown how to figure out* by themselves *what is important to ask and how they can find answers, clarify concepts, and remember later what they read.*

*Ruth liked this idea and began teaching Lynn how to ask her own questions. She did this by modeling the questioning technique she used. Soon, they both became encouraged by the progress Lynn was making.*

■  ■  ■

When you ask all the questions, you decide what is important for your student to know, not your student. Your student learns how to answer your questions, but doesn't learn how to figure out what is important to ask in the first place. Active questioning is a learned skill. Just as you were taught how to do it earlier in this chapter by means of a model questioning pattern, you also must teach your student to generate his or her own questions by providing a model.

Modeling is a basic technique of comprehension training. It provides direct instruction in the *process* of active comprehension. The idea is to show your student your own strategies for comprehending what you read. To do this, you read aloud for your student and pause periodically. During the pause, you evaluate your comprehension and demonstrate what you do when you encounter difficulties. You must think aloud as you pose questions for yourself and come up with answers, clarify concepts you find difficult, and develop stategies to remember what you have read.

Here are three comprehension training models you can use—one for asking and answering questions, one for clarifying concepts, and one for learning how to remember. Train your student in each model in three stages, over three to six sessions. Spend at least one session on each stage, as follows:

Stage 1: Model the tasks for the student by doing all the reading and all the activities yourself.

Stage 2: Slowly phase yourself out by giving the student more and more of the activities to do. Guide the student's practice, sometimes doing the activities with him or her. Be sure to provide encouragement and feedback and keep the student on track.

Stage 3: Let the student practice independently by doing all the reading and all the activities alone.

## Model for Active Questioning Training

1. Read a sentence or paragraph from the session's reading selection.

2. Ask yourself a general question about the material. It should be a broad question and cover either the material itself or your thoughts about it. Don't use any simple, direct recall questions.

3. Decide if the answer to the question can be found in the text or if you must use prior knowledge.

4. Then either find the answer or figure it out yourself.

5. Tell how you arrived at your answer.

6. Go on to the next sentence or paragraph and continue the training for the next 20 minutes.

## Model for Active Clarifying Training

1. Read a sentence or paragraph from the session's reading selection.

2. If you understand it, make a fist and put your thumb up. Go on to the next sentence or paragraph.

3. If you don't understand it, make a fist and put your thumb down.

4. Decide if you don't understand what you read because you are having difficulty with the definition of a word or phrase, or with the content as a whole.

5. Reread the material to figure out the unknown definition or to understand better what the author is saying. Ask another person to help you clarify the material.

6. Go on to the next sentence or paragraph and continue the training for the next 20 minutes.

## Model for Active Remembering Training

1. Read a sentence or paragraph from the session's reading selection.

2. Summarize it in your own words.

3. Figure out what parts are important to remember. Make a note of these if you wish.

4. Predict what the author will say in the next paragraph.

5. Go on to the next paragraph and continue the training for the next 20 minutes.

6. When you stop, summarize all of what you have read.


Now practice your own comprehension modeling technique in Practice Problem 2–8.

PRACTICE PROBLEM 2–8: Comprehension Training Models
Use the following complex sentence to practice your comprehension training technique. Fill in the comprehension training models below.

The process of learning has been defined . . . as the extraction from confusion of meaningful patterns; input can be thought of as the *raw material* of that confusion: what is perceived by the individual that bears on that particular pattern in any way.*

*From *Human Brain and Human Learning* by Leslie A. Hart. Longman, New York and London, 1983, p.70.

### Active Questioning Training

Ask a broad question about the reading. _____
_____

Decide if the answer can be found in the text or if you must figure it out. _____

Find or figure out the answer. _____
_____

Explain your line of reasoning. _____
_____
_____

### Active Clarifying Training

Assume that there is something you don't understand in the reading. Decide if the problem is with a word, a phrase, or with the whole thing. _____
Reread and discuss the reading to clarify difficult parts.
_____
_____

### Active Remembering Training

Summarize the reading. _____
_____

Decide what is important to remember. _____
_____
_____

Predict what will come next. _____
_____

You will find a sample solution to this practice problem on page 126.

---

*Checklist Review*

---

## Active Questioning Training

1. Read a sentence or paragraph.
2. Ask a broad question about it.
3. Decide if the answer can be found in the text or if you must figure it out.
4. Find or figure out the answer.
5. Explain your line of reasoning.
6. Go on to the next sentence or paragraph.

## Active Clarifying Training

1. Read a sentence or paragraph.
2. Put your thumb up if you understand it. Then continue reading.
3. Put your thumb down if you don't understand it.
4. Decide if the problem is with a word, a phrase, or with the whole thing.
5. Reread and discuss the reading to clarify the difficult parts.
6. Go on to the next sentence or paragraph.

## Active Remembering Training

1. Read a sentence or paragraph.
2. Summarize it.
3. Decide what is important to remember.
4. Predict what will come next.
5. Go on to the next sentence or paragraph.
6. Summarize all of what you've read.

# Comprehension Through Study Skills

*Case Study*

*Peter, a 25-year-old carpenter, wanted to get a high school equivalency diploma. Once he had his diploma, he could take the contractor's licensing exam. While he could read and understand short stories and newspapers, Peter was at a loss when it came to studying textbooks. And he would have to do a lot of studying for the exam.*

*Gary, Peter's reading tutor, found a textbook on carpentry that he and Peter could use to develop his study skills. In the process of going through the book, both Peter and Gary learned a great deal that was new to them about carpentry.*

■  ■  ■

Study skills are refined comprehension skills. Essentially, they include the ability to recognize, separate, and prioritize information and ideas in text material, and then to remember everything for future testing. Good study techniques make reading an active process in which the reader brings to the reading all of his or her background knowledge on the topic. Good study skills help the reader organize new information as it relates to information already possessed.

Instruction in study skills is appropriate for any student who reads above the fourth-grade level. It becomes increasingly important for students at higher reading levels and for students who must read textbooks.

## The SQ3R Study Skills Technique

The *SQ3R: Survey, Question, Read, Recite, Review* study skills technique developed at Cornell University is considered by major university reading programs to be very effective. This technique is described here. If it is used with each of your student's readings, you will see dramatic improvement in the student's ability to retain complex written information and ideas.

There are three phases in the SQ3R study skills technique. First, your student *surveys* (S) the reading. Then, the student asks *ques-*

*tions* (Q) about individual subsections, *reads* (R) the subsections, and *recites* (R) their content. Finally, your student *reviews* (R) the reading as a whole. Here is how the technique works in more detail.

SURVEY
Surveying provides an overview of the reading, similar to an aerial photo of a landscape. It helps the student establish topics and categories into which new facts and ideas can be fitted. Surveying means looking over the reading, as a whole or by section, to see what it is about. In the SQ3R technique, it involves reading the title, headings and subheadings, and the first and last paragraphs of each subsection. Then the reader glances at the illustrations and makes note of the general layout.

QUESTION
Questioning necessitates reading purposefully for answers rather than reading without direction. In the SQ3R technique, it involves first reading the headings and subheadings, and then changing those headings and subheadings into questions. The questions can be written in a notebook, with space left below each one for filling in the answers later. Questions provided at the end of the reading or following the sections or chapters should also be included.

READ
Reading extracts the main ideas and details from the material. It becomes an active process in which the student focuses on information and ideas that relate to the questions developed earlier for each heading and subheading. In the SQ3R technique, it involves reading the material under the headings and subheadings, one paragraph at a time, and separating the contents into main ideas and details.

RECITE
Studies have shown that reciting is the most effective means for improving retention of reading material. In the SQ3R technique, the student covers up the material under each heading and subheading after reading it. Then the student recites in his or her own words the information and ideas it contains. Finally, the student answers the

questions he or she drafted for that material. The student may also want to take notes on points to remember.

REVIEW
The reviewing phase rebuilds the reading into a recognizable whole. In the SQ3R technique, the student reflects on the entire reading by looking at its construction. Then the student thinks about what has been learned about the topic, decides whether he or she agrees with the conclusions of the reading, and determines what generalizations can be drawn from it.

Now practice your own study skills technique in Practice Problem 2–9.

PRACTICE PROBLEM 2–9: SQ3R Study Skills Technique
Use the SQ3R study skills technique to survey Chapter 3, which starts on page 128. Be sure to glance at the lists and lesson plan samples. Then turn each heading and subheading into a question. List your questions here. Later, after you have read the chapter, come back and answer your questions.

_____

_____

_____

_____

_____

_____

_____

_____

_____

_____

_____

You will find a sample solution to this practice problem on page 127.

| Checklist Review | |
|---|---|
| SQ3R Study Skills Technique | |
| S = Survey | Survey the reading as a whole or by section. |
| Q = Question | Change each heading and subheading into a question. |
| R = Reading | Read the material under each heading and subheading to answer the question. |
| R = Recite | Recite the information and ideas learned under each heading and subheading. |
| R = Review | Review the reading as a whole. |

# Sample Solutions to Practice Problems in Part 3, Chapter 2

PRACTICE PROBLEM 2–1: Selecting Reading Topics

1. Read through the Reading Topics List on the preceding pages.

2. List the four topic categories that interest you most.

   *Health Care*
   *Injustices*
   *Interpersonal Relations*
   *Technology*

3. Write the topic categories in the order of your personal interest in reading about them.

   1st choice: *Health Care*
   2nd choice: *Interpersonal Relations*
   3rd choice: *Injustices*
   4th choice: *Technology*

4. Read through the subtopics listed in the category you picked as your first choice. List the three subtopics that interest you most.

*CPR*

*jogging*

*medical Technology*

5. Which of these subtopics would you like to read about first?

*jogging*

If you were being tutored, your tutor would begin by finding reading materials on this subtopic.

PRACTICE PROBLEM 2–2: Using Your Library

List three library resources that will help you find information on the topic you decided most interested you in Practice Problem 2-1 on page 74.

1. *Subject card catalog*
2. *Reader's Guide to Periodical Literature*
3. *Librarians*

PRACTICE PROBLEM 2–3: Writing Down Material

Use the space below to write down the following paragraph to the third-grade level.

1. Rewrite the paragraph by shortening the sentences, substituting short words for long ones, and omitting unimportant words and phrases.
2. Mark off the first 100 words of your new paragraph.
3. Count the number of sentences.
4. Count the number of syllables.
5. Check the chart to see if your new paragraph is approximately at the third-grade level.
6. If necessary, adjust the length of sentences and words  even more to bring the paragraph down to the third-grade  level.

**Original Paragraph**

In the beginning, you may be intimidated by the thought of writing down a paragraph to a lower level. Perhaps you think there is a "correct" way of doing it. No, fortunately, there is no correct way. There is only a correct procedure. First, you must shorten the long sentences. Take out all the introductory clauses and write simple subject-predicate sentences. Next, you must substitute short words for long ones and omit unimportant words and descriptive phrases. Don't worry if the meanings of words change slightly. Sometimes such adjustments are unavoidable. The task, you see, is really not very complicated. Just do the best you can. You can practice by writing down this paragraph.

**Your Paragraph**

At first, you may think it's too hard for you to write something down to a lower level. Maybe you think there is a "right" way of doing it. There isn't a right way, only a right approach. First, shorten the sentences. Take out beginning clauses that aren't needed. Write simple sentences. Next, use short words for long ones. Don't use extra words or long phrases to describe things. Don't worry if you change the meaning a little. Sometimes you can't help it. Just do the best you can. It's really not very hard. You can practice with this paragraph.

This written-down paragraph has 100 words, 13 sentences, and 127 syllables. According to the chart on page 77, it is written at the low third-grade level.

PRACTICE PROBLEM 2–4: Brainstorming
Take the topic that most interested you in Practice Problem 2–1 on
page 74 and expand it as set forth in this section. Below is a chart to
fill in using your topic.

Topic: _Jogging_

| Historical/Political | 1. History of jogging<br>2. Famous people who jog<br>3. Legends and stories |
| --- | --- |
| Economic/Material | 1. Running equipment<br>2. Cost of training<br>3. Finding the time |
| Psychological/Personal | 1. Physical fitness / dangers<br>2. Stress reduction<br>3. Personal satisfaction gained |
| Social/Cultural | 1. Group runs<br>2. Peer pressure to run<br>3. Opinions of nonjogging friends |
| Scientific/Technological | 1. Best times of day<br>2. Training methods<br>3. Healing running injuries |
| Religious/Spiritual | 1. Mental preparation<br>2. The "runner's high"<br>3. Running and meditation |

PRACTICE PROBLEM 2–5: Activities Flowchart
Fill in this simplified activities flowchart using an item from the topic
you brainstormed in Practice Problem 2–4, page 82.

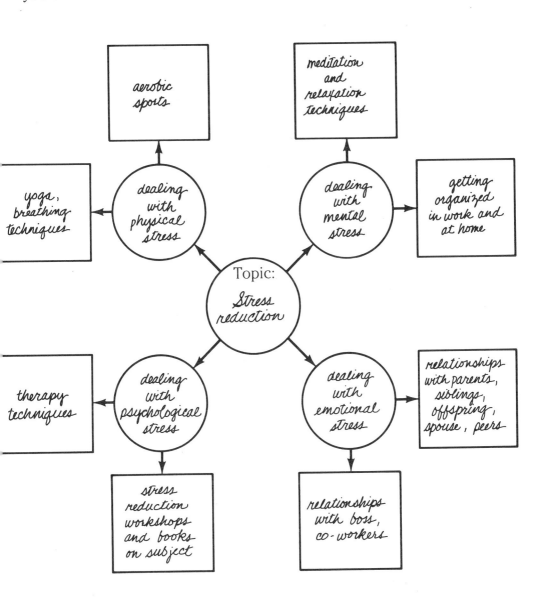

PRACTICE PROBLEM 2–6: Questioning Pattern
Read the following excerpt from a short story on nurse's aides*
written at the third-grade level. Then write one sample for each type
of question.

> Jean got up and turned off the TV. Then she went back to
> the sofa. Cindy, her friend, was sitting there. Cindy's face looked
> sad. But Jean had a big smile on her face.
> 
> "Don't you just love movies about hospitals?" Jean asked.
> "Life, death, health, sickness—so much goes on. It's all so
> important. It's never boring. I want to work in a hospital."
> 
> "That's just a TV show," Cindy said. "It's just a movie. It's
> not like that in a real hospital. All you saw were the pretty things.
> The drama. You didn't see all the ugly things. The bed-wetting.
> The people who can't feed themselves. The ones who yell at
> you."
> 
> Cindy hated hospitals. She knew what they were like.
> Watching people die wasn't pretty.

*From *Drama at the Hospital* (Career Reader No. 1—Nurse's Aide) by Nadine Rosenthal. David S.
Lake Publishers, Belmont, Calif. (1986).

## Literal Recall Questions

1. Describe: *What did Jean and Cindy just finish doing?*

2. Reorganize: *Compare Jean's and Cindy's attitudes.*

## Interpretive Questions

3. Analyze: *Why do you think Cindy had such strong
negative feelings about hospitals?*

4. Generalize: *From this short passage, how would you
describe Jean's and Cindy's personality types?*

## Active Questions

5. React: *How do you feel personally about hospitals?*

6. Act: *Would you ever work in a hospital?
Why or why not?*

PRACTICE PROBLEM 2–7: Comprehension Activities
Reread the short story excerpt about hospitals in Practice Problem 2–6
on page 95. Then, from each set of comprehension activities, choose
one activity that would help someone comprehend the excerpt. Adapt
the activities to the excerpt and write them in the spaces below.

Literal Recall Activities

Describe: *Remove every tenth word from the selection. Then
have the student read the altered selection, putting in
the deleted words in whatever way seems to make sense.*

Reorganize: *Help the student make a chart contrasting
Jean's and Cindy's views about hospitals.*

Interpretive Activities

Analyze: *Tell what this passage means: "Cindy hated
hospitals. She knew what they were like.
Watching people die wasn't pretty."*

Generalize: *Have the student list three possible
outcomes of the story and then select the
outcome he or she likes best.*

Active Activities

React: *Add the students and my own opinions
about hospitals to the chart made above.*

Act: *Have the student rewrite the story,
substituting himself or herself for Cindy.*

Oral Fluency Activity

*Make a dramatization of the reading. One of us will
read Jean's lines, and the other will read Cindy's lines.
We'll try to say our lines with real feeling.*

PRACTICE PROBLEM 2–8: Comprehension Training Models
Use the following complex sentence to practice your comprehension training technique. Fill in the comprehension training models below.

The process of learning has been defined . . . as the extraction from confusion of meaningful patterns; input can be thought of as the *raw material* of that confusion: what is perceived by the individual that bears on that particular pattern in any way.*

*From *Human Brain and Human Learning* by Leslie A. Hart. Longman, New York and London, 1983, p.70.

### Active Questioning Training

Ask a broad question about the reading. *What is the process of learning?*

Decide if the answer can be found in the text or if you must figure it out. *In the text*

Find or figure out the answer. *Learning is figuring out meaningful patterns from confusing raw material.*

Explain your line of reasoning. *The answer is stated in the sentence, but I had to reread it several times to understand it precisely. The punctuation was especially difficult.*

### Active Clarifying Training

Assume that there is something you don't understand in the reading. Decide if the problem is with a word, a phrase, or with the whole thing. *The whole thing*

Reread and discuss the reading to clarify difficult parts. *To extract is to take. So take a confusing statement and develop meaningful patterns from it. Use the input (raw material) or anything that helps you to figure out patterns.*

### Active Remembering Training

Summarize the reading. *The process of learning is detecting meaningful patterns from confusing things.*

Decide what is important to remember. *To learn, we must take meaningful patterns out of the confusing raw materials presented to us.*

Predict what will come next. *An example of how patterns are detected in confusing input.*

PRACTICE PROBLEM 2–9: SQ3R Study Skills Technique
Use the SQ3R study skills technique to survey Chapter 3, which starts
on page 128. Be sure to glance at the lists and lesson plan samples.
Then turn each heading and subheading into a question. List your
questions here. Later, after you have read the chapter, come back
and answer your questions.

1. What does word recognition have to do with learning to read?

2. What are sight words? How do I build my student's sight word vocabulary? What are some good sight word activities?

3. What is phonics? What is the phonics teaching sequence? What are some good phonics activities?

4. What is syllabication? What are the syllabication rules? What are some good syllabication activities?

5. What is language experience? What is the language-experience procedure? How do I carry out a language-experience lesson?

6. How can I build my student's vocabulary? What activities are good to use?

7. How can I help to improve my student's spelling? How can I find good spelling words? What are the basic spelling rules? What is a good technique to teach spelling?

8. How do I teach writing to an intermediate student? What are some good writing activities to use?

**Chapter 3**

 *Learn to Read: Word Recognition*

> *"Reading to learn" focuses*
> *on grasping the meaning of*
> *print. "Learning to read"*
> *focuses on decoding print*
> *and must be placed within*
> *the context of "reading to*
> *learn."*

Although a reading's content might be quite interesting to your student, he or she may not be able to recognize the words in it with any degree of ease. At first, you may be overwhelmed by just how much difficulty your student has with even the simplest words. You may feel unprepared for the task of helping him or her acquire basic word-recognition skills. But as with anything else, you will be unprepared only until the task is broken down into manageable steps. Then you can identify the problem areas and prepare remedial activities.

This chapter first presents the four major methods for teaching word recognition. Three of these—the sight-word, phonics, and syllabication methods—are word centered. They focus on improving word-by-word reading by using a controlled vocabulary to teach a sequence of distinct reading skills.

The fourth word-recognition teaching method, commonly called language experience, is used only for beginning reading students. In this method, you write the personal experiences dictated by your student, and then the student reads the stories back to you. Because the student reads words in a context that is familiar and meaningful, both comprehension skills and word-recognition skills are improved with this method.

The last part of this chapter offers guidelines and activities for improving your student's vocabulary, spelling, and writing skills. Don't hesitate to add your own ideas to those presented in the text. You will often pick up on individual needs and problems that a general coverage such as this has not included.

# Sight Words

*Case Study*

*Mel's student Mary had great difficulty hearing the differences between vowel sounds. To Mary, short a sounded like short e, and short e sounded like short i. Mel tried a variety of short-vowel and letter-sound drills, but the techniques all proved fruitless.*

*When she came to their session one night, Mary related to Mel a detailed account of everything she had seen on her way there. At the time, Mel paid little attention. After a few more exasperating drills, however, he remembered Mary's account. He decided to use Mary's strong sight memory to build her word-recognition skills. He selected whole words, rather than letter sounds, from Mary's verbal account and put them on flash cards. Because the words were taught in a familiar context, Mary was able to recognize them. Her word-recognition skills began to improve from that lesson on.*

■　■　■

Words that we are able to read instantly, without sounding them out letter by letter or syllable by syllable, are called "sight words." These are words we see often in our daily lives. Because we all have vocabularies of differing sizes and varying facility with word recognition, each of us has a unique sight-word vocabulary.

The sight-word method of reading instruction teaches people to read words as whole units. This is an especially good method for helping students master common words that are not phonically regular, such as *said, of,* and *does.* It is also good for teaching people who have difficulty discriminating between the different sounds in a word. Discrimination difficulties are especially common among speakers of nonstandard English and those for whom English is a second language. These people's verbal speech patterns don't contain certain sounds found in standard English. (See the article *Nonstandard English* in Part 4, page 203.)

Student: _____*Sharon*_____   Lesson Number: ___5___

Level: _____*2nd*_____   Date: _____*10/7*_____

1. Reading Topic (*30* minutes)

   *Health and nutrition. I got a few health-food books from the library. One seems straightforward and organized into clear-cut topical chapters. I summarized the introduction to the book in a single simple page and typed it up. I'll read each sentence, then Sharon will read the sentence again.*

2. Questions (*20* minutes)

   *Why is nutrition important to health?*
   *Why are so many Americans undernourished?*
   *Are you surprised that the number is so high? Why?*
   *What does the author say we can do about it?*
   *Discuss if each of us thinks we are undernourished according to the author's guidelines.*

3. Comprehension Activities (*20* minutes)

   ■ *Ask Sharon what three facts in the reading are the most important to remember. I'll write them down as she says them. Then I'll cut them apart and have her read and prioritize them.*
   ■ *Have Sharon make up a title for the reading based on the three facts.*

4. Word-Recognition Activities (*20* minutes)

   *The word **food** comes up often in the reading, so I'll use it for today's word-recognition activity. I made a chart to drill her, omitting the **oo** words that rhyme with **book**.*

| | | | | |
|---|---|---|---|---|
| *food* | *cool* | *boom* | *soon* | *hoop* |
| *mood* | *fool* | *room* | *moon* | *coop* |
| *brood* | *stool* | *doom* | *noon* | *loop* |
| | *school* | *broom* | *spoon* | *stoop* |
| | *pool* | *gloom* | | *troop* |
| | | *groom* | | *droop* |

5. Vocabulary, Spelling, and Writing Activities (*30* minutes)

- *Give Sharon the spelling words from last week and choose words from the above chart for her to study this week.*
- *Since the word* **undernourished** *appears in the reading, I'll ask her what it means. Then I'll give her more words beginning with* **under-** *and ask for their meanings; for example, underarm, underground, underline, undersell, undershirt. I'll write the meanings she gives me, and then she will copy them.*

6. Evaluation and Suggestions for Next Session

- *Sharon is very interested in nutrition, so it will be our topic for a while.*
- *She liked the* **under-** *exercise, so we also generated words beginning with* **over-**.
- *She missed both* **stool** *and* **stoop**.
- *Next time: Use more prefixes for vocabulary building. Review* **st-***words.*

Student: _____Ross_____    Lesson Number: _____5_____

Level: _____4th_____    Date: _____4/14_____

## 1. Reading Topic (35 minutes)

*Educational computer games. I found a review in this Sunday's newspaper of several educational games for home computers. Ross will preview the article using SQ3R, and then read it with my help. I will start him on active questioning training by showing him how to ask questions and figure out answers for three sentences in the article.*

## 2. Questions (10 minutes)

*What educational computer games does the article review?*
*What criteria does it use to review the software?*
*Do any of the games sound good to you? Why or why not?*
*What would make an educational game interesting for you?*
*Would you like to try out any kinds of educational computer games? If so, what kinds?*

## 3. Comprehension Activities (25 minutes)

*Make a chart of the criteria used in the article to review the games. Add other criteria that Ross thinks are important. Then tell how each game meets or fails to meet the criteria.*

|             | Game 1 | Game 2 | Game 3 |
|-------------|--------|--------|--------|
| Criterion 1 |        |        |        |
| Criterion 2 |        |        |        |
| Criterion 3 |        |        |        |
| Criterion 4 |        |        |        |
| Criterion 5 |        |        |        |

4. Word-Recognition Activities (*20 minutes*)

■ *Review the words Ross stumbled over. If any of them follow the syllable rules, we'll review them.*

■ *Look for words in the article ending in* -tude *and* -tute; *for example, aptitude and substitute. Brainstorm more words with those endings, including at/ti/tude, grat/i/tude, sol/i/tude, in/sti/tute, and con/sti/tute. Note the long* u *and the silent* e *in the ending and apply the syllable rules to the rest of each word.*

5. Vocabulary, Spelling, and Writing Activities (*30 minutes*)

■ *Ask Ross which three words he wants to learn from the reading to build his vocabulary. Tell him to write a sentence for each word for next week.*

■ *Have Ross write one sentence to describe each game. We'll analyze each one to determine if the sentence is complete or not and why. I've used a simple grammar book to help me write some incomplete sentences for him to complete.*

■ *I bought a small book with blank pages for him to use to keep a journal. He should write one page a week.*

6. Evaluation and Suggestions for Next Session

■ *Ross definitely wants to check out education games.*

■ *The grammar book was a good idea. It gives me lots of ideas for exercises.*

■ *He said he would try the journal, but he wasn't too confident.*

■ *Next time: See if the library has a computer and educational games for public use.*

# Building a Sight-Word Vocabulary

In order to read even the simplest printed copy, a person must be able to recognize 200 to 300 basic words. A starter list of 280 such words is given on pages 136-137. Add to it other, more difficult words that would be appropriate as sight words for the topic your student wants to read about. For example, a student who wants to read about handling stress would benefit from a sight-word familiarity with the words *stress, anxiety, relax, tension,* and *control.* Your student may also ask to learn words that are necessary for daily living, such as *bus, address, schedule,* or words used on the job. Getting words orally from your student and giving them back in written form is a sure way to build reading vocabulary.

## STARTER LIST OF 280 BASIC SIGHT WORDS

| | | | | |
|---|---|---|---|---|
| about | black | down | go | if |
| after | blue | drink | goes | in |
| again | both | each | going | into |
| all | boy | eat | good | is |
| almost | bring | end | got | it |
| also | but | even | great | it's |
| always | buy | every | green | just |
| am | by | face | grow | keep |
| an | call | fall | had | kind |
| and | came | family | hand | know |
| any | can | far | has | large |
| are | car | fast | have | last |
| around | carry | few | he | left |
| as | children | find | head | less |
| ask | city | first | help | let |
| at | clean | five | her | life |
| ate | cold | fly | here | light |
| away | come | for | high | like |
| back | could | found | him | little |
| be | cut | four | his | live |
| because | day | friend | hold | long |
| become | dear | from | home | look |
| been | did | full | hope | love |
| before | didn't | funny | hot | made |
| began | do | gave | house | make |
| best | does | get | how | man |
| better | done | girl | hurt | many |
| big | don't | give | I | may |

| | | | | |
|---|---|---|---|---|
| me | over | show | this | were |
| money | own | side | those | what |
| more | part | since | three | when |
| most | people | sing | time | where |
| much | pick | sit | to | which |
| must | place | six | today | while |
| my | play | sleep | together | white |
| myself | please | small | told | who |
| name | pretty | so | too | why |
| need | pull | some | took | will |
| never | put | soon | try | wish |
| new | ran | start | two | with |
| next | read | still | under | woman |
| nice | red | stop | until | work |
| night | ride | such | up | world |
| no | right | take | upon | would |
| not | room | tell | us | year |
| now | round | ten | use | yes |
| of | run | than | used | you |
| off | said | thank | very | your |
| old | same | that | walk | |
| on | saw | the | want | |
| once | say | their | warm | |
| one | school | them | was | |
| only | see | then | wash | |
| open | seem | there | water | |
| or | set | these | way | |
| other | seven | they | we | |
| our | she | thing | well | |
| out | should | think | went | |

## Sight-Word Activities

Incorporate the following sight-word activities into lessons when your student is reading. They can be especially valuable for building his or her reading vocabulary.

■ Have the student begin a dictionary of personal sight words. Then he or she can add words learned from each reading.

■ Underline five sight words that relate to the topic of the reading. As the student comes to each underlined word, have him or her make a flash card for it.

■ Before the student reads a selection, ask him or her to skim through it to identify unknown words. Make a list of the words to analyze later.

■ For sight words that can be illustrated, make flash cards with words on the front and pictures on the back.

■ Ask the student to make sentences using the words on three sight-word flash cards.

■ Flash a stack of five sight-word cards at the student, slowly at first and then faster until he or she can read all the cards rapidly. Add cards to the stack as your student learns more words, and delete cards as the student learns the words.

■ Categorize some of the new sight words alphabetically, by meaning, by sound similarity, and/or by part of speech.

■ Spread some flash cards on a table with the sight words facing up. Have the student find words as you say them.

■ Deliberately mispronounce some of the words on the flash cards and have your student catch the mispronunciations.

■ Make up crossword puzzles for some of the sight words.

Now use Practice Problem 3–1 to practice developing sight-word activities.

PRACTICE PROBLEM 3–1: Sight Words
The first ten words from the basic sight-word list are listed below.
Review the sight-word activities and then describe how you would
use three of them with these words.

| about | almost | am |
|-------|--------|-----|
| after | also | an |
| again | always | and |
| all | | |

1. _____

_____

_____

_____

2. _____

_____

_____

_____

3. _____

_____

_____

_____

You will find a sample solution to this practice problem on page 187.

# PHONICS

### Case Study

*Mike, Carole's 40-year-old literacy student, could understand and discuss anything that was read to him. But he could read only a few words by himself. He had a very good memory for what he heard but a poor memory for what he saw.*

*When he was a child, Mike's teachers had used readers that focused on teaching sight words; he had very little phonics instruction. Carole began a strict phonics curriculum to teach him how to sound out words systematically. She integrated phonics exercises into readings that were interesting to him, and the approach worked. Slowly but surely, Mike began learning to read.*

■ ■ ■

The phonics method of reading instruction uses a set of rules and generalizations to teach the sounds that single letters and letter combinations make when read aloud. Because English borrows from many languages, there are many exceptions to its phonics rules and generalizations. In spite of the exceptions, however, phonics is a valuable method of teaching reading. It is especially valuable for teaching people who remember what they hear better than what they see and for giving all learners clues on how to read unknown words.

While there is no single correct way to teach phonics, its principles are taught in a standard sequence, noted on pages 141–145. This sequence will lead your student step-by-step toward a recognition of basic one-syllable words.

Often, new tutors ask how long they should continue teaching one phonics principle before going on to the next. The answer is straightforward—stay with one principle long enough to teach it thoroughly without boring your student. Then return to it later for review and reinforcement and also for comparing it with other principles. Review and reinforcement are always valuable, since seeing and working with patterns many times are what lead to easy recognition. And comparing principles with one another helps make better sense of all of them.

If your student reads at or below the second-grade level, it's best to follow the total sequence of phonics principles. If the student reads at or above the third-grade level, concentrate on teaching the principles in which he or she was shown to be weak by the RDPA.

## Sequence for Teaching Phonics Principles

1. **Single consonants.** *Teach single consonants as they occur in the beginning position of three-letter words.*

2. **Short vowels.** *Teach short vowels as they occur in the middle of three-letter words.*

The easiest order in which to learn short-vowel discrimination is *a, i, o, e, u.* Start by teaching words with short *a*, then short *i*, and then discriminate between them. Add words with short o, and then discriminate between them and the words with short *a* and short *i*. Add words with short *e* and then short *u*, discriminating between each one and the words with the three other short vowels.

One-syllable words that have the same ending and rhyme all belong to the same word family. Go through the alphabet to find beginning consonants to use with the word families below. Then generate three-letter words; for example, -*ab:* cab, dab, gab, jab, lab, nab, tab.

| -ab | -ib | -ob | -ed | -ub |
| --- | --- | --- | --- | --- |
| -ad | -id | -od | -eg | -ug |
| -ag | -ig | -og | -en | -um |
| -am | -in | -op | -et | -un |
| -an | -ip | -ot | | |
| -ap | -it | | | |
| -at | | | | |

3. **Beginning blends.** *Teach beginning blends as they occur at the beginning of one-syllable words with short vowels.*

Blends are combinations of two or three consonants, each with a distinct sound that blends smoothly with the other(s). Use the beginning blends below with the list of word families above to generate four- and five-letter words; for example, -*ap:* clap, flap, slap, snap, trap, scrap, strap.

| l *blends* | r *blends* | s *blends* | 3-*letter blends* |
|---|---|---|---|
| bl- | br- | sc- | scr- |
| cl- | cr- | sk- | spl- |
| fl- | dr- | sm- | spr- |
| gl- | fr- | sn- | squ- |
| pl- | gr- | sp- | str- |
| sl- | pr- | st- | |
| | tr- | sw- | |

**4. End Blends.** *Teach end blends as they occur at the end of one-syllable words with short vowels.*

Mix beginning consonants and beginning blends with the end-blend word families below to generate four- and five-letter words; for example, -*and:* band, hand, land, sand, bland, gland, brand, grand, strand.

| l *blends* | n *blends* | t *blends* | *others* |
|---|---|---|---|
| -all | -and* | -ant | -ass |
| -alm | -ang* | -art | -amp* |
| -ill* | -ank* | -ast | -iss |
| -old* | -ing* | -ift* | -oss |
| -oll* | -ink* | -irt | -omp |
| -ell | -int | -ist | -ess* |
| -elp* | -ond* | -ort | -ump* |
| -ull | -ong | -ost | |
| | -end* | -eft | |
| | -end | -elt | |
| | -ung* | -est* | |
| | -unk* | -ust* | |

*most common three-letter word families

**5. Beginning and end digraphs.** *Teach digraphs in the beginning and end position of one-syllable words with short vowels.*

Digraphs are combinations of two consonants that produce a totally different sound than either of them has separately. The most common digraphs are *sh*, *th*, and *ch*. Use beginning digraphs with the word families above to generate four- and five-letter words; for example, shin, thin, chin; shell, chest, theft. Then mix beginning consonants, beginning blends, and beginning digraphs with the word families below to generate four- to six-letter words; for example, *-ash:* bash, cash, dash, gash, hash, lash, mash, rash, clash, slash, brash, crash, trash, smash, stash, splash. (Note that when *ch* follows a short vowel, a *t* or *r* is added before it.)

| -ash | -ish | -osh-oth | -esh | -ush |
| --- | --- | --- | --- | --- |
| -ath | -ith | -otch | -etch | -utch |
| -atch | -itch | -orch | -erch | -urch |
| -arch | -irth | | | |

**6. Long vowels with silent e.** *Teach this rule: The silent* e *at the end of a word makes the vowel before it say its name.*

Mix beginning consonants, beginning blends, and beginning digraphs with the word families below to generate four- to six-letter words; for example, *-ade:* fade, jade, made, wade, blade, glade, grade, spade, shade.

| -ace | -ice | -ode |
| --- | --- | --- |
| -ade | -ide | -oke |
| -age | -ife | -ole |
| -ake | -ile | -one |
| -ale | -ine | -ope |
| -ame | -ite | -ote |
| -ape | -ive | |
| -ate | | |

**7. Long vowels in two-vowel combinations.** *Teach this rule: When two vowels go walking, the first one does the talking (and says its name).*

Mix beginning consonants, beginning blends, and beginning digraphs with the word families below to generate four- to six-letter words; for example, *-eek:* leek, meek, peek, reek, seek, week, sleek, creek, cheek.

| *long* a | *long* e | *long* e | *long* o |
|---|---|---|---|
| -aid | -each | -eed | -oach |
| -ail | -ead | -eek | -oad |
| -ain | · -eak | -eel | -oam |
| -ait | -eam | -eem | -oan |
| -ay | -ean | -eep | -oat |
|  | -eat | -eet |  |

**8. Miscellaneous vowel combinations.** *Teach the various sounds of the most common vowel combinations: oi, oo, ou. Don't bother to teach more unusual combinations or any of the numerous exceptions to the rules. Your student will pick those up naturally as his or her reading skills improve.*

Mix beginning consonants, beginning blends, and beginning digraphs with the word families below to generate four- to six-letter words; for example, *-ook:* book, cook, hook, look, nook, took, brook, crook, shook.

| | | |
|---|---|---|
| -oil | -ook | -ound |
| -oin | -oom | -our |
| -oint | -oon | -ouse |
| -oist | -oop | -out |
|  | -oot |  |

**9. Vowels controlled by *r, l,* and *w.*** *Teach this rule: When a vowel is followed by* r, l, *or* w, *it takes on a unique sound.*

Mix beginning consonants, beginning blends, and beginning digraphs with the word families below to generate four- and five-letter words; for example, *-ark:* bark, dark, hark, lark, mark, park, spark, shark.

| -ar | -ird | -ald | -aw |
|-----|------|------|-----|
| -ard | -irt | -alk | -awn |
| -arm | -or | -eld | -ew |
| -arn | -ord | -elt | -ow |
| -art | -ork | -ild | -own |
| -er | -orn | -old | |
| -ern | -ur | | |
| -ir | | | |

10. Contractions. *Teach this rule: Some words are joined together and shortened so they will be easier to say.*

When letters are taken out, an apostrophe is put in their place. There are six major contractions: *'t, 'd, 's, 'll, 've, 're.* Here are some examples of them: would not/wouldn't, he would/he'd, what is/what's, I will/I'll, we have/we've, we are/we're.

---

*Checklist Review*

### Phonics Sequence

1. Single consonants
2. Short vowels
3. Beginning blends
4. End blends
5. Beginning and end digraphs
6. Long vowels with silent *e*
7. Long vowels in two-vowel combinations
8. Miscellaneous vowel combinations
9. Vowels controlled by *r, l,* and *w*
10. Contractions

## Phonics Activities

These phonics activities will be helpful for students who read at the first- to third-grade level.

■ First dictate letters to your student to write. Then dictate letter sounds and have him or her write the letters.

■ Make a list of words in the same family and have the student read them in the order they were written. Then have the student read them randomly as you point to them. Finally, have the student use three of the words in one sentence.

■ Have the student read into a tape recorder a list of words in the same family. Listen for the rhyming sound while playing it back.

■ Make a set of cards, one inch square, for the alphabet. Use them for the following activities.

—Spread five consonant cards and one vowel card on a table and ask your student to use them to make as many three-letter words as possible. Write the words on paper. Then designate blends and digraphs for four- to six-letter words. Add a second vowel and start another round.

—Lay out several word families and five beginning consonants and have the student make words from them.

—Have the student paste or draw a picture on the back of each card that shows something that begins with that letter.

—Put the cards in a box and have your student draw them out one at a time, say the letter and the sound it makes, and then give a word that starts with that letter.

—Ask your student to make sentences with the words named above.

—Point to a card and say a sound. Ask the student to tell you if you said the correct sound. If not, tell him or her to correct you.

—Have the student alphabetize the cards.

■ Make flash cards for all the words in a family. Give your student three of the cards to study and say aloud. Next, have the student close his or her eyes while you take away one card. Then have your student tell you which one is missing. Repeat with other sets of three or more cards.

■ Make flash cards for several word families. Use single consonants from your set of alphabet cards to make three-letter words in each family. Have your student say, spell, and write words, and then use them in sentences.

■ Make a list of blends and digraphs on the left side of a piece of paper and a list of word families on the right side. Have your student make words by drawing lines from the blends and digraphs to the endings.

■ List several words on a piece of paper. Then manipulate them in the following ways for the student to read aloud.

—Substitute a vowel, as in *fat* and *fit*.

—Reverse the order of the letters, as in *pets* and *step*.

—Insert a letter between others, as in *pup* and *pump*.

—Add letters at either end, as in *rip, trip,* and *trips*.

—Start with a vowel and add various letters anywhere to make new words, as in *a, at, bat, brat,* and *brats*.

■ Say, "I'm thinking of a word. It rhymes with (bag) and it (waves in the air). What is it?" (flag). Use words with phonics elements that your student is currently learning.

■ Take turns with the student, pointing to objects in the room that are spelled with a particular beginning consonant, blend, or digraph.

■ Say four short-vowel words—three that rhyme with each other and one that does not. Have the student tell you the one that does not rhyme. Do the same thing with long-vowel words.

■ Write a short story using as many words as you can from the same word family. Have the student read it and tell you the family. Then he or she can make up another story with the same family.

■ Bring in a newspaper and have your student circle the words that contain the phonics element he or she is trying to learn.

## Phonics Games for Adults and Adolescents

■ Adapt commercial word games such as Scrabble, Spill and Spell, Anagrams, Bingo, and Boggle to your purposes.

■ Make up at least two bingo cards with phonics elements you are teaching—for example, beginning or end blends. Then prepare whole-word flash cards with the blends. Let the student read the flash cards as the two of you cover the corresponding blends.

■ Make up a dominoes game by cutting 3″ x 5″ cards into thirds lengthwise. Across one side of each domino, draw a line to divide it in half. Then make two matching sets by marking letters, blends, digraphs, and words in the domino sections. Have your student play by finding matching dominoes and laying them side by side. Then ask him or her to make up words or sentences using the matched elements.

■ Play tic-tac-toe with your student, but instead of using Xs and Os, each of you chooses a beginning blend. Then fill in the squares with words that start with your blends.

■ Make up simple crossword puzzles of words with the phonics element your student is currently learning.

■ Wastebasketball: Cut out squares of newspaper and circle one word on each square that contains the phonics element your student is learning. If your student reads a circled word correctly, he or she gets one point; if he or she wads up the square of newspaper and throws it successfully into the wastebasket, he or she gets another point. When it's your turn, you can read your word correctly or incorrectly. If the student catches you reading it incorrectly, he or she gets the point.

## Phonics Activities for Nonreaders

■ Cut out letters of the alphabet from sandpaper. Then have the student trace them with his or her finger and print them on paper.

■ As you draw a letter on your student's back, have him or her draw it on paper.

■ If a chalkboard is available, have the student write letters on it using a motion that utilizes the whole arm.

■ Have your student trace letters you have written.

■ Make up alphabet flash cards with letters on the front and pictures on the back of things that start with the letters. Drill these flash cards in alphabetical order, then randomly. Increase speed as your student becomes more proficient.

■ Say the names of letters to your student and have him or her say the sounds. Then say the sounds and have the student say the letters.

■ Print three short words, all beginning with the same letter, on a piece of paper. Have the student read the words and identify the beginning sound.

Now practice developing phonics activities with Practice Problem 3–2.

PRACTICE PROBLEM 3–2: Phonics
Read the following selection from a short story written at the third-grade level.* Then do the activities listed below the reading.

Mark Nelson sat on the park bench. It was fall. The wind blew past Mark's face. He looked up at the trees. The leaves were changing colors. The trees were a mass of orange and yellow. Mark could look at those trees for hours. At least it was something to do. He was waiting for Rita. And Rita was always late. . . .

Mark lit a cigarette. Just then, Rita walked up. "Why don't you quit smoking?" she asked Mark. Rita had quit the month before. Now she was after Mark to do the same.

*From *Looking Good* (Career Reader No. 6—Beauty Operator) by Nadine Rosenthal. David S. Lake Publishers, Belmont, Calif. (1986).

1. Find two small words with short *a* and two words with long *a*/silent *e*. List them here.

    Short *a* words                     Long *a*/silent *e* words

    _____          _____

    _____          _____

    Develop a phonics activity for one of the four words you listed above. Refer to the lists on pages 146–147.

    _____

    _____

    _____

    _____

2. Find one word that has *ee* in it and one word that has *ea* in it. List them here.

    Vowel-combination *ee* word   Vowel-combination *ea* word

    _____          _____

    Develop a phonics activity for one of the vowel-combination words you noted above. Refer to the lists on pages 146–147.

    _____

    _____

    _____

    You will find a sample solution to this practice problem on page 188.

# Syllabication

---

*Case Study*

*Stephanie's student Todd had just graduated from high school, but he still had trouble sounding out words of more than one syllable. He tended to look at the first letter or the first syllable and then guess the word. At first Stephanie encouraged Todd's guessing. She knew that predicting what comes next is important to comprehension. Soon, however, she realized that he was guessing wildly without any strategy. So she began showing him how to break words into manageable chunks. Todd's word recognition improved tremendously after a few months and so did his reading comprehension.*

■  ■  ■

In phonics, one-syllable words are sounded out. Syllabication, however, focuses on breaking long words into syllables so that they can be read more easily. A syllable is a word part with one vowel sound, regardless of the number of actual vowels in it. Two vowels in a syllable need not be located next to each other, but they must form only one vowel sound between them, as, for example, the *i* and *e* in like/ly. Syllabication also leads easily into work with roots, prefixes, and endings. A root is a basic meaning unit to which prefixes and endings can be added to change its meaning.

If your student can read one-syllable words fairly well, he or she has probably mastered basic sight words and phonics, or perhaps needs only a cursory review. The student can be assumed to read at the high third- or fourth-grade level. Now it is time to expand his or her word recognition with instruction in how to break down multi-syllabic words into readable parts. The six basic syllabication rules below will help you.

## Syllabication Rules

1. Compound words. If there are two words in one, divide between the words; for example, with/out, some/one, some/where.

2. V̆C/CV. If there are two consonants between two vowels, divide between the consonants. The first syllable in such constructions is called a "closed" syllable because the vowel is closed off by the consonant that follows it. The vowel takes on its short sound; for example, căm/pus, măg/net, vĕl/vet.

3. V̄/CV or V̆C/V. If there is only one consonant between vowels, first try dividing before the consonant. Since the vowel is at the end of the first syllable, it is called "open." It takes on its long sound; for example, fī/nal, mū/sic, hō/tel. If the word does not sound right when divided this way, try dividing it after the consonant. Since the vowel is then closed, it takes on its short sound; for example, săt/in, căb/in, lĕm/on. In English, 60 percent of VCV words divide before the consonant and 40 percent after it.

4. **Words ending in *le*.** If a word ends in *le*, count back three letters from the end to find the final syllable; for example, săm/ple, stā/ble, rī/fle.

5. **Prefixes and endings.** A prefix or ending is its own word part, as in pre/pay, re/run, fit/ness, cold/er, mis/in/form/a/tion, un/like/ly.

6. **Blends and digraphs.** Treat blends and digraphs as single consonants for the purpose of breaking words into syllables; for example, con/trol, com/plete, ham/ster, re/place, fur/ther.

---

*Checklist Review*

Syllabication Rules

1. Compound words: some/day
2. V̆C/CV: pen/cil
3. V̄/CV or V̆C/V: ho/tel or lem/on
4. Words ending in *le:* sam/ple
5. Prefixes and endings: un/sure and sure/ly
6. Blends and digraphs: con/trol and fash/ion

---

## Syllabication Activities

The following activities will provide your student with effective drill on syllabication, prefixes, and endings.

■ Make a list of words with prefixes and have the student draw a line between the prefixes and roots. Discuss how the prefixes change the meanings of the roots.

■ Make a list of difficult words in the reading and have the student break them into syllables.

■ Select common nouns and add the endings *-er, -or,* and *-ist* to create job titles; for example, teach/teacher, conduct/conductor, science/scientist.

■ Select a root and have the student add prefixes and endings to it.

■ See how many words the student can make from a list of compound words, such as somewhere, nowhere, everywhere, everybody, somebody, nobody, someone, everyone.

■ Select common verbs and add the endings *-s* or *-es, -ed,* and *-ing.* Discuss how the endings change the meanings of the verbs.

■ Select common adjectives and add the endings *-er* and *-est* to them. Discuss how the endings change the meanings of the root words.

■ Make a list of multisyllabic words and have the student count the syllables in each one.

■ Take the multisyllabic words your student misreads, put them on a separate piece of paper, and do the following with them.

—Analyze which syllable rules they follow and why. Then categorize them according to rules.

—Analyze which words have similar prefixes or endings. Then categorize them accordingly.

—Analyze which words have similar prefixes or roots. Then generate more words with the same prefixes or roots.

■ Have the student look up in a dictionary the words he or she misreads and notice the way they are syllabicated. Then ask him or her to tell why they are divided that way.

■ Say, "I'm thinking of a word. It has three syllables and means _____ . What is it?" Use multisyllabic words that were discussed previously in your session.

■ Take one paragraph from the text your student is going to read and have him or her break all the multisyllabic words into syllables beforehand.

■ Have the student underline all the vowels in a sentence. Then have him or her break the multisyllabic words into syllables following the rule that each syllable has only one vowel sound even though it may have more than one vowel.

■ Have the student put words that were missed while reading onto flash cards, breaking the words into syllables.

Now practice developing syllabication activities with Practice Problem 3–3.

PRACTICE PROBLEM 3–3: Syllabication

1. Identify eight two-syllable words in this section on syllabication
   that adhere to the V̆C/CV rule. (Don't include the examples that
   are given.)

   _____       _____

   _____       _____

   _____       _____

   _____       _____

2. Develop a syllabication activity for the words noted above. Use
   the list on pages 152–153 to help you.

   _____

   _____

   _____

   _____

You will find a sample solution to this practice problem on page 189.

# Language Experience

*Carolyn was tutoring Diana, a 48-year-old woman who had difficulty reading even the simplest words. They were reading a very low-level adult basal reader about two men who worked in a factory. The book described how big the factory was, the jobs the men did, and how much they liked their work. The story was dry, and Diana did not agree with its point of view. She worked in a factory and had very different feelings about it.*

*Carolyn asked Diana to talk about her own experiences in the factory. As Diana spoke, Carolyn wrote what she said, using Diana's words. Diana described what she did each day and how boring her work was. But she said it was the only job she could get, and she had children to feed. She then talked about finding a better job once she had learned to read.*

*Carolyn helped Diana read back her own story. Then they made flash cards of the difficult words for Diana to study at home. Finally, Carolyn helped Diana copy the story into her notebook. An otherwise dull lesson was saved.*

■   ■   ■

Sight words, phonics, and syllabication develop word-recognition abilities on a word-by-word basis. These methods are useful with students who already have some reading skills. But the language-experience method of instruction works best with very low-level readers. It relies on stories your student generates about his or her own experiences rather than on published low-level materials or readings that you prepare. You put the oral language of the story into its printed form, and the student as author can see his or her own words on paper. Since these are the very words that your student said aloud, he or she has a good chance of being able to read them back. When doing this, the student learns how to translate written symbols back into oral language.

## Language-Experience Procedure and Topics

Here are ten steps to follow for working through a language-experience lesson. This is an active and engaging procedure that both of you should find stimulating. The list of topics included will give you and your student some ideas in case you encounter difficulty in selecting a topic.

1. Find a topic that is personally exciting to your student. There is often one obvious topic that he or she is interested in. But sometimes it is necessary to discuss various topics for a while until you can narrow them down to one.

2. Have the student dictate what he or she knows about the topic as well as his or her thoughts and feelings on it. If necessary, keep asking questions to draw out information.

3. Print the story exactly as the student tells it, whether or not the grammar is standard. Be sure to keep the story short.

4. Read the story with your student. Do it one word or one sentence at a time if necessary. Repeat each segment as often as you think will help.

5. Have the student read the story alone. Don't rush, and help when he or she seems really stuck. But don't jump in too quickly. Allow time for remembering and figuring out.

6. Ask your student questions about the story. Perhaps he or she will want to change something in it or add something to the story from the answers.

7. Pull out sight words and word families from the story. Make flash cards and lists of unknown words for your student to drill with.

8. Have the student copy the story into a notebook.

9. Help the student correct the copy and then ask him or her to read it aloud to you.

10. Type the story to use for review during the next session.

TOPICS FOR LANGUAGE-EXPERIENCE STORIES
- past experiences from your own life
- a sports team or event
- photos of family and friends
- photos of places visited

- wishes
- fears
- feelings
- lies you have been told
- strange events you have witnessed
- interview
- television and movie plots
- newspaper stories
- comics
- customs
- work and work situations
- mistakes you have made
- funny times
- hard times
- changes you would make in your life
- letter writing
- children
- home life
- family history
- current events
- something that happened today
- travels or vacations
- hobbies
- cooking

---

*Checklist Review*

**Language-Experience Procedure**

1. Choose a topic with your student.
2. The student dictates a story to you.
3. You print the story.
4. Your student reads the story back with your help.
5. The student reads the story alone.
6. You ask the student questions about the story.
7. You work with the student on sight words, word families, and unknown words from the story.
8. The student copies the story in a notebook.
9. The student corrects the story and rereads it.
10. You type the story for review during the next session.

---

# A Sample Language-Experience Lesson

Here is how Carolyn worked with Diana to create a language-experience lesson. The first section scripts their dialogue. Then comes the story itself and sample drill material.

Carolyn: So you didn't think the factory story was very real, hm? Tell me about your factory job.

Diana: Well, I go to work every day on time. You have to be on time or they would dock your pay and you wouldn't get paid and things would get real nasty.

Carolyn wrote: *I go to work every day on time. You have to be on time or they dock your pay. You wouldn't get paid. Things would get real nasty.*

Carolyn: Do you like your job in the factory?

Diana: No way. No one likes a factory job. They're real boring. All I do is strip plastic ends from these wires.

Carolyn wrote: *No way do I like that factory job. No one likes a factory job. They're real boring. All I do is strip plastic ends from these wires.*

Carolyn: Is there any other job you could have gotten?

Diana: Jobs are hard to come by. Especially if you can't read. I have to feed my kids, you know. How can you go looking for a job when you have to feed your kids? Tell me that.

Carolyn wrote: *I couldn't have gotten another job. Jobs are hard to come by. Especially if you can't read. I have to feed my kids, you know. How can you go looking for a job when you have to feed your kids? Tell me that.*

Carolyn: I don't know. It's a real problem. Anyway, here's what you just said. Now I want you to read it back to me.

MY FACTORY JOB

by

Diana

I go to work every day on time. You have to be on time or they would dock your pay. You wouldn't get paid. Things would get real nasty.

No way do I like that factory job. No one likes a factory job. They're real boring. All I do is strip plastic ends from these wires.

I couldn't have gotten another job. Jobs are hard to come by. Especially if you can't read. I have to feed my kids, you know. How can you go looking for a job when you have to feed your kids? Tell me that.

- Sight words for drill

  From list on pages 136–137: work, every, have, would, one, come, your

  From student's own vocabulary or basic to topic: nasty, factory, boring, plastic, wires, strip, another, especially

- Phonically regular words for drill

  short *i*: -*id* as in *kids*: bid, did, hid, lid, mid, rid, Sid, slid, grid, skid, squid

  short *i*: -*ip* as in *strip*: dip, hip, lip, nip, rip, sip, tip, zip, blip, clip, flip, slip, drip, grip, trip, skip, snip, ship, chip

  long *i*: -*ime* as in time: dime, lime, mime, slime, crime, grime, prime

  long *i*: -*ike* as in *like*: bike, hike, Mike, pike, spike, strike

  long *a*: -*aid* as in *paid*: laid, maid, raid, braid

  long *a*: -*ay* as in *pay*: bay, day, hay, jay, Kay, lay, may, nay, ray, say, way, clay, play, slay, gray, pray, tray, stay, sway, spray, stray

Now use Practice Problem 3–4 to practice your knowledge of the language-experience procedure.

PRACTICE PROBLEM 3–4: Language Experience

Without looking back, list the ten steps for the language-experience procedure.

_____

_____

_____

_____

_____

_____

_____

_____

_____

_____

_____

_____

You will find a sample solution to this practice problem on page 189.

# Vocabulary Building

*Case Study*

*Julie and her 17-year-old student Bobbie decided they were both going to work on building their vocabularies. Each week they both brought in three words they wanted to learn— words they had read or heard someone else say. After telling each other their words, they used a dictionary to check meanings they weren't sure of. Then they tried to slip their own words into the conversation without the other one noticing. They got a dollar of Monopoly money for every word they successfully slipped past each other. Whoever had less money at the end of three months took both of them out for dessert. Then they started another round.*

■ ■ ■

Words are building blocks of knowledge. A good vocabulary helps us think clearly and logically and communicate our thoughts in a powerful and convincing manner to others. It allows us to move our eyes and mind over a page of print with speed and understanding. To comprehend the spoken and written thoughts of others, we must be able to grasp the exact meanings of their words.

Many people believe that vocabularies grow naturally with age. Actually, the opposite is generally true. We might develop a large vocabulary while attending school, but we only use a limited number of words in our daily lives. If we don't use words, we lose them.

Reading, of course, is one means for building vocabulary because it introduces us to many new words. But if we fail to learn the words and use them, they won't become part of our vocabularies.

The importance of helping your student build a strong vocabulary cannot be overstated. When you ask a question about a reading and he or she searches for the words to describe thoughts and information, you know it's time to work on vocabulary. If your student is a low-level reader, vocabulary building is more a function of listening and speaking than of reading and writing. Poor readers use many more words in their speech than they are able to read.

Student: _____Sharon_____　Lesson Number: ___6___

Level: _____2nd_____　Date: ___10/14___

1. Reading Topic (*30 minutes*)

    *Nutrition. In the adult new readers' section at my local library, I found a very simple book on nutrition. It's written at the second-to third-grade level. Sharon will read the first chapter this week.*

2. Questions (*10 minutes*)

    *What kinds of foods are in each of the basic food groups?*
    *Why are too many carbohydrates bad for you?*
    *Which nuts and grains are good sources of protein?*
    *Why is too much red meat bad for you?*
    *Do you want to eat less red meat? Why or why not?*

3. Comprehension Activities (*20 minutes*)

    *We'll make a chart together showing each basic food group and the good and bad things about eating foods in that group.*

|  | *Good Things* | *Bad Things* |
|---|---|---|
| *Carbohydrate* |  |  |
| *Protein* |  |  |
| *Fat* |  |  |

4. Word Recognition Activities (*30 minutes*)

    ■ *Since Sharon needs a review of **st-** words, we'll begin with **starch** from the reading. I'll give her these words to read: stab, stack, stand, step, stick, sting, stop, stock, stub, stud. Then she has to come up with more **st-** words.*
    ■ *We'll play blend tic-tac-toe. Sharon will use a red pen, and I'll use a blue one. We'll fill in squares with **st-** words after using them first in sentences.*

5. Vocabulary, Spelling, and Writing Activities (*30 minutes*)

- *Sharon will give me definitions for* **carbohydrate, protein,** *and* **fat.** *I'll write her definitions; then she'll read them and copy them.*
- *Give her the spelling words from last week.*

6. Evaluation and Suggestions for Next Session

- *The food groups were confusing for her, and so was the chart.*
- *The tic-tac-toe was a good exercise. It got her thinking.*
- *Next time: Work more with blends. She has a hard time with them. Work with each food group separately for the next three weeks.*

Student: _____ *Ross* _____    Lesson Number: _____ 6 _____

Level: _____ *4th* _____    Date: _____ *4/21* _____

1. Reading Topic (*20* minutes)

*Educational computer games. My local library has a computer and a few educational games. Ross will read the manual for one of the games and then play it. I reserved the computer for the second half of our lesson. I'll take one sentence and show him how to apply active question training to it, as we did last week.*

2. Questions (*10* minutes)

*What is the object of the game?*
*What are the rules?*
*What is the educational value of this game?*
*Does it seem interesting or boring to play? Why?*
*Do you think something that is educational should also be fun?*
   *Why or why not?*

3. Comprehension Activities (*60* minutes)

*Ross will play the game. He has used a computer to play regular video games, but not educational games. Nor has he used this particular computer before. I'm familiar with it, however, so I can help him.*

4. Word-Recognition Activities (*0* minutes)

*The word-recognition activity is part of the game. It's a game on breaking words into syllables and is meant for nine-year-olds, but the game is not insulting for an older player to use.*

5. Vocabulary, Spelling, and Writing Activities (*30 minutes*)

   ■ *Ross will write what he liked and disliked about the educational computer game. He must come up with two arguments each for and against such games. I'll correct for spelling and complete sentences. I'll use another drill from my grammar book.*

   ■ *Ask him about his journal writing. Give him encouragement. Ask to see his three sentences using vocabulary words from last week. Choose three more words from the game manual for him to use this week.*

6. Evaluation and Suggestions for Next Session

   ■ *The computer game went very well. It's a good drill of syllables, but that's all. We decided to use it next time, too. But Ross still wants to read more, not just use the computer. We didn't have time to do the writing activity.*

   ■ *Next time: Get him a library card and a book to start reading, perhaps from the children's novel section or the adult new readers' section. Also, there are books on computer literacy for kids. Maybe he'll be interested in one of those.*

## Vocabulary-Building Methods

Here are six methods for developing your student's vocabulary.

**1. Building word lists.** Many commercial vocabulary-building books boast, "Fifteen minutes a night to a better vocabulary." They give word lists, word games, and word puzzles. You can adapt this method to give your student short practice sessions with new words in the readings.

**2. Finding word origins.** Finding the origins of words is a good way to begin vocabulary development. Dictionaries usually give this information. Work with your student to look up new words. Explain the language derivations and the way words change from language to language and over time.

**3. Analyzing prefixes and roots.** Sixty percent of English words are formed of roots with prefixes. When your student comes across a common prefix and/or root form, write the word on a sheet of paper. Then generate more words, first with the prefix and then with the root. List them on the paper. Discuss the definitions and the relationship of the words to each other.

Here are some common prefixes and roots.

| Prefix | Meaning | Root | Meaning |
|--------|---------|------|---------|
| anti | against | cede, cess | go, yield |
| auto | by itself | cred | believe |
| bi | two | duc | lead |
| dis | take apart, not | fact, fect | do |
| ex | out of | grad, gress | go, walk, stop |
| im | not | graph | write |
| in | into, not | mit, mis | send |
| inter | between | pass, path | feel |
| micro | small | pel | push |
| mis | wrong | pend | hang, think |
| poly | more than one | port | carry |
| pre | before | prin, press | press, squeeze |
| re | again | quer, ques | ask, seek |
| semi | half | reg | direct, lead |
| sub | under | spec | see, look |
| super | great | spire | breathe |

*(continued on next page)*

| Prefix | Meaning | Root | Meaning |
|--------|---------|------|---------|
| tele | far away | thermo | heat |
| trans | across | tract | draw, pull |
| un | not | vert, vers | turn |

**4. Developing the dictionary habit.** Tell your student to keep a small dictionary handy and use it when an unknown word crops up. Try to make sure the student uses the word in a sentence or in conversation with you. Then have him or her write it in a personal dictionary.

**5. Getting familiar with the thesaurus.** Have your student jot down words he or she comes up with when in a pinch to find the "right" word, then bring the words to the next session. Together, look up the words in a thesaurus to find synonyms. Let your student write a few of the synonyms on a piece of paper to practice in sentences or in conversation with you.

**6. Using the frontier system.** The frontier system is the most personalized system of vocabulary building. A person's frontier words are the ones he or she is familiar with but doesn't know well enough to use. The frontier system divides words into these three categories.

> *Known words:* Words a person uses often in daily speech and writing. They are not part of vocabulary-building endeavors.
>
> *Somewhat known words:* Words a person understands when read or heard but seldom uses because their precise meanings or pronunciations aren't familiar. Motivation to learn these words is high since they have been read or heard in a meaningful context. **These are a person's frontier words.**
>
> *Unknown words:* Words that hold no meaning for a person even when read or heard. These words are beyond a person's frontier. They should be saved to learn later.

When your student comes across personal frontier words, have him or her jot them down. Work together to look the words up in the dictionary. Then have the student write them in sentences. Spend time discussing synonyms, antonyms, and roots and prefixes. Make a game out of using the words with each other during this and the next lesson.

---

*Checklist Review*

### Vocabulary-Building Methods

1. Building word lists
2. Finding word origins
3. Analyzing prefixes and roots
4. Developing the dictionary habit
5. Getting familiar with the thesaurus
6. Using the frontier system

---

## Vocabulary Activities

These activities should be used together with the preceding vocabulary-building methods.

■ Collect five frontier words from discussion and readings and do the following with them.
—Make flash cards with the words on one side and the definitions on the other.
—Make flash cards with the words on one side and synonyms and antonyms on the other.
—See which of you can use the words first in conversation.
—See which of you can use the words without the other one realizing it.
—Give a definition and have the student say the word for it.
—Put the words into a personal dictionary.
—Make a crossword puzzle with the words.
—Look the words up in the dictionary to find meanings and origins.
—Look the words up in a thesaurus.
■ Write a frontier word so the student can't see it and do the following with it.
—Have the student guess the word from hints you give.
—Have the student ask yes/no questions to guess the word.
—Give the student a word that rhymes with the word and have him or her guess it.
—Give the student a synonym or antonym and have him or her guess the word.

■ Use a word from the reading that is formed with a root and prefix and do the following with it.

—Brainstorm other words with the same root and prefix.

—Use the word in sentences.

—Discuss the meaning of the word.

—Put the word into a personal dictionary.

—Make flash cards of this root and this prefix, as well as other roots and prefixes. Then mix and match them to form words.

■ Pick a word from the reading that your student doesn't know and do the following with it.

—Analyze how the word was used in the sentence.

—Generalize the definition of the word from the general context of the sentence.

—Look to see if the definition of the word is actually given in that sentence or the next one.

—See if an example of the word comes later in the sentence.

—See if a restatement of the word comes later in the sentence.

—See if the word is compared or contrasted with other words later in the sentence.

Now use Practice Problem 3–5 to practice generating a vocabulary-building lesson yourself.

PRACTICE PROBLEM 3–5: Vocabulary Building
Read the following paragraph on beauticians,* and then find the root
for each of the five words listed below. Generate more words that
use the root in combination with various prefixes and suffixes.

Beauty operators, also called *beauticians, hairstylists,* or
*cosmetologists,* care for customers' hair, hands, nails, and skin.
They give permanents and lighten or darken the color of hair.
They may give manicures and scalp and facial treatments, apply
makeup, and clean and style wigs.

*From *Teacher's Guide for The Career Readers* by Nadine Rosenthal. David S. Lake Publishers,
Belmont, Calif. (1986).

1. operators: _____

_____

2. beauticians: _____

_____

3. cosmetologists: _____

_____

4. manicures: _____

_____

5. facial: _____

_____

You will find a sample solution to this practice problem on page 190.

# Spelling

*Case Study*

*Frank was tutoring Myra, a 36-year-old woman who read fairly well. But because her spelling was so poor, Myra had a block against writing. She spelled phonically and came up with some odd word variations; for example,* wurk *for* work, cawfee *for coffee, and* nikul *for nickel. To get her over this reliance on phonics, Frank started Myra on a program of sight-word spelling. He encouraged her to look closely at the words she read and to pick out some that held special interest for her. These he made into word lists for focused study and used them in writing drills. Slowly, Myra began to feel more confident and to enjoy the writing activities.*

■  ■  ■

Spelling requires the ability to remember the sequence of letters in words. It involves practice in memorization and visualization techniques as well as some knowledge of orthographic patterns. This last skill makes use of the pattern-detecting nature of the brain.

Your student knows that people are judged harshly for poor spelling. Like Myra, he or she probably believes that the best way out is to avoid spelling altogether. So it's very possible that even if your student reads at the sixth-grade level, he or she has done very little writing, since spelling and writing are inseparable.

Spelling instruction, therefore, must be placed in the context of writing. Never rely solely on spelling lists and spelling workbook exercises. Be sure also to take meaningful words from the student's reading and own writing endeavors. Expand on those words with words that are similar in meaning or sound. Then have the student use the words in writing activities. Until they are used, the words won't be learned.

You may want to use the RDPA to test which phonics elements the student finds difficult to spell. Instead of asking the student to read the words on the lists, have him or her spell them as you dictate each one and use it in a sentence. Use the evaluation forms to record and analyze the results. Then find or make word lists that incorporate the problem phonics elements. Give five to ten of these words a week for home study.

## Sources of Spelling Words

Five major sources of spelling words are noted here. Decide on the best sources for your student's particular needs. Then use those sources in each session to build and reinforce your student's spelling skills.

1. **Word families.** After teaching a misspelled word from your student's writing, brainstorm a list of words that belong to the same family. Assign five of the words to study at home for the next session.

2. **Sight words.** Misspelled sight words from your student's writing will not necessarily fit into any pattern, so they must be learned separately. Put them on flash cards for drill. Work also with other sight words from the basic list on pages 136–137.

3. **Topic words.** Work with misspelled words from your student's writing that are related to the student's reading topic. These words may be more difficult than those he or she would normally use, but they're part of the topic of interest and should be learned.

4. **Homonyms.** Use misspelled homonyms (words that sound alike but have different spellings and meanings) to teach the meanings as well as their spellings. Some common homonyms are given here.

| | | | |
|------|-----------|-------|----------------|
| be | bee | one | won |
| by | buy, bye | peace | piece |
| brake | break | red | read |
| dear | deer | right | write |
| eight | ate | sea | see |
| foul | fowl | sight | site, cite |
| great | grate | son | sun |
| hall | haul | stair | stare |
| heal | heel, he'll | steak | stake |
| hear | here | steal | steel |
| hour | our | their | there, they're |

*(continued on next page)*

| loan | lone | | threw | through |
| knot | not | | to | too, two |
| maid | made | | weight | wait |
| mail | male | | wood | would |
| main | mane | | your | you're |
| meat | meet | | | |

**5. Spelling rules.** If your student consistently misspells words that follow one of the four basic spelling rules, teach the rules.

*The doubling rule:* If a one-syllable word has one short vowel and one consonant at the end, double the final consonant before adding an ending that begins with a vowel; for example, stop/stopping and plan/planned, but not mean/meaner and milk/milked.

*The final e rule:* If a word ends in a silent *e*, drop the *e* before adding an ending that starts with a vowel; for example, use/using, dance/dancer, and fame/famous, but not place/placement and care/careful.

*The y to i rule:* If a word ends in a consonant plus *y*, change the *y* to *i* before adding an ending except *-ing*; for example, ready/readiness, lucky/luckily, and duty/dutiful, but not study/studying.

*The ie-ei rule:* Put *i* before *e* except after *c* or when pronounced as *ay* as in neighbor and weigh; for example, believe, friend, and achieve, but not vein or freight.

---

| *Checklist Review* |
|---|
| **Sources of Spelling Words** |
| 1. Word families |
| 2. Sight words |
| 3. Topic words |
| 4. Homonyms |
| 5. Spelling rules |

## A Flash-Card Spelling Technique

Many poor spellers have never been shown a good technique for learning such spelling aids as separating the sounds within a word and visualizing a word as a whole. The technique detailed here can help if your student doesn't yet use such aids for spelling. Adapt it to suit his or her abilities. Begin by using both auditory and visual stimuli; then add the tactile stimulus if necessary.

1. Make up a flash card for each problem word.
2. Your student looks at the flash card and says the word slowly, listening to the sounds in it.
3. The student spells the word aloud while looking at it.
4. Turn over the flash card so the student can spell the word aloud without looking at it.
5. Your student looks at the flash card to correct any misspelling.
6. Turn over the flash card again, and the student writes the word.
7. The student looks at the flash card once more to correct any misspelling.
8. After three written misspellings, put the card aside for later drill.
9. Begin the process again with a new word, but start by having the student trace the letters in the word with a finger while spelling it aloud.
10. After three correct written spellings, consider the word learned. Throw out the card.

## Spelling Activities

The purpose of spelling instruction is to help your student gain mastery over the spelling process. These activities can be used to supplement the flash-card technique.

■ Place the flash card across the room. Have the student walk up to it, look at the word carefully, and then walk back to the table and write it.

■ Have the student write each spelling word in a sentence.

■ Make a list of the spelling words and leave blank spaces where single or double vowels go. Then ask the student to fill in the blanks.

■ List the spelling words and have the student write a word in the same family for each one.

- Have your student write a story using ten of the spelling words.
- Ask the student to list the spelling words alphabetically.
- Tell the student to write each spelling word and circle the vowels.
- Have the student list the spelling words from shortest to longest.
- Have your student find all the little words in a spelling word; for example, father contains fat, at, the, he, her.
- Ask the student to add a prefix or a suffix to a spelling word and then discuss its changed meaning.
- Play hangman with the spelling words.
- Make up a word-search puzzle with the spelling words.
- Classify the spelling words; for example, one-syllable words, two-syllable words, words that start with a consonant, words that start with a vowel, words that have a long vowel, and so forth.

Now practice remembering the spelling rules and techniques with Practice Problem 3–6.

PRACTICE PROBLEM 3–6: SPELLING

1. List three words that follow each of the four spelling rules discussed in this section.

   The doubling rule

   _____    _____    _____

   The final *e* rule

   _____    _____    _____

   The *y* to *i* rule

   _____    _____    _____

   The *ie-ei* rule

   _____    _____    _____

2. Without looking back, list the ten steps in the flash-card spelling technique.

   _____

   _____

   _____

   _____

   _____

   _____

   _____

   _____

   _____

   _____

   _____

   _____

   _____

   _____

You will find a sample solution to this practice problem on pages 190–191.

# Writing

---

### Case Study

*Pearl had tutored LeeRoy for six months before he agreed to begin writing in a serious manner. Up until then, he'd made excuses whenever she had given him a writing assignment.*

*After consulting with a writing teacher, Pearl decided to have LeeRoy write stories from his life. For the first one, she told him to describe a person who had affected his life as a young boy and what that person had done. She told him not to worry about grammar or spelling but just to get his thoughts down. To her surprise, LeeRoy actually did it. They reworked the story several times over the next month, until they were both satisfied with it. During the next six months, LeeRoy wrote three more stories and made them into a book. He gave the book to his wife for her birthday.*

■   ■   ■

Consider the intermediate student who reads above the sixth-grade level but writes at the fourth-grade level. That student lacks the confidence and skills needed to overcome a long-standing mental block against writing. When he or she attempts to write, hand and brain refuse to cooperate. Or a page of words may be produced, but the words may make little sense. Your first task is to provide support for a student such as this, so that he or she can gain some writing confidence. Encourage the student to write on topics he or she feels comfortable with. And since writing is a skill that is best learned by doing, avoid workbook exercises except as supplementary drills.

If your student can write half a page (even if it's incoherent) on a topic you name, then use the following sequence to build writing skills. Later, if writing becomes a major activity in your sessions, you may also want to find a simple grammar book or a book on teaching writing in the library or bookstore.

## Sequence for Developing Writing Skills with Intermediate Writers

1. Prewriting. Prewriting is the most neglected stage of the writing process. Without gathering and sorting thoughts before writing, your student will produce only simple, poorly constructed essays and stories.

The prewriting steps vary according to the purpose of the writing: descriptive, narrative, or expository. The descriptive essay describes something by its looks, feel, smell, sound, or taste. The narrative tells a story of events or experiences. The story may be fiction or nonfiction and may occur in the past, present, or future. The expository essay uses statements and opinions to explain what is known about a topic. The prewriting steps, adapted according to the kind of writing to be done, are given here.

*Presenting a stimulus:* For a descriptive essay, present a visual stimulus such as a photo, a drawing, or an object. For a narrative, provide oral stimulus through discussion of childhood, parents, schooling, friends, siblings, crises, good times, and other experiences. For an expository essay, use a written stimulus such as a newspaper or magazine article, a story, or a cartoon.

*Gathering ideas:* Have your student gather ideas by generating nouns and verbs or phrases that describe the stimulus. Have him or her write each word or phrase on a separate 3″ x 5″ card. You may also have the student generate adjectives and adverbs that describe each of the original words. Add these words to the appropriate cards.

*Clustering ideas:* Have your student sort the 3″ x 5″ cards into three or four categories, write a title for each category on another card, and place that card on top. Then have the student put the cards from each category into a good order for writing about them.

2. Writing. Your student is now ready to begin writing a first draft. This is exploratory writing. Therefore, it is done without worrying about paragraphing, sentence structure, grammar, punctuation, erasures, or scribbles. Do have the student try to spell all words correctly and underline those words he or she thinks are probably misspelled.

*Writing a topic sentence:* Help your student write a topic sentence. It should incorporate the category titles and the order of ideas developed during the prewriting activities. You can do this by asking your student a question whose answer is a listing of the category titles and the order of ideas for the writing. The answer thus becomes the topic sentence.

*Writing the first draft:* Now have the student write an essay or narrative that develops each category into a paragraph. The result of this should be three or four paragraphs that each relate back to the topic sentence. The words and phrases generated on the 3"x 5" cards should be used to help add substance to each paragraph. A conclusion sentence should wrap up all the ideas in the draft.

3. **Revising**. Sometimes it's difficult to figure out where to begin correcting a student's writing. There may be no sense of paragraphing or sentence structure; the grammar and punctuation may be incoherent; and the spelling may be unintelligible. But focus your first comments on *what* is written rather than on *how* it's written. Give positive feedback on and discuss the ideas and creativeness in the writing. Have the student read it aloud to you. Many students will catch missing facts, words, and punctuation as they do this.

Next, help your student work on paragraph development, sentence structure, grammar, capitalization and punctuation, and spelling. The best way to do this is to have him or her correct the errors. Limit your suggestions so that you don't overwhelm the student. Tell him or her what to change and help with doing it. If there isn't enough time for the student alone to make all the corrections, correct some of the writing yourself. (Don't use red pencil.) Then explain why you are making the changes. Here are the elements to focus on at this stage.

*Paragraph development:* A paragraph is a group of sentences that develops one central thought. It begins with a topic sentence that conveys the main idea, followed by detail sentences that tell why or how the topic sentence is true. Often, a final sentence either closes the paragraph or provides a transition to the next paragraph.

*Sentence structure:* A sentence is a group of words that expresses a complete thought. It must be about something (the subject or actor) and what that something is doing (the predicate or action). Most sentence errors are either run-on sentences (two or more sentences running into each other) or sentence fragments (incomplete sentences that have only subjects or predicates).

*Grammar basics:* The basic parts of speech are nouns and pronouns, adjectives, verbs, adverbs, conjunctions, and prepositions. Nouns are names of persons, places, or things. Pronouns are words that are used in place of nouns. Adjectives are words that modify nouns and pronouns. Verbs are words that express action. Adverbs are words that are used to modify verbs, adjectives, or other adverbs. Conjunctions are words used to join words, phrases, clauses, or sentences. Prepositions are words used to show the relation of a noun or pronoun to some other word in the sentence.

*Capitalization and punctuation:* Capital letters are used to begin sentences. They are also used for proper nouns (the names of people, organizations, geographical places, events, nations, nationalities, races, religions, and so forth). Capitals are also used in the titles of books, television shows, movies, magazines, and so forth. Periods, exclamation points, and question marks end the various types of sentences and indicate long pauses when reading. Commas, on the other hand, indicate short pauses. They are used to separate the items in a series, before conjunctions in long compound sentences, and to set off long phrases at the beginning of sentences and parenthetical interrupters in the middle. The best comma rule is "When in doubt, leave it out." If you find the need to explain more advanced punctuation marks such as the colon, semicolon, and dash, a good writing handbook can give some pointers.

*Spelling:* Correct misspelled words by either having your student look them up in the dictionary or supplying the spelling yourself. Keep a list of misspelled words and use the activities suggested in the preceding spelling section to work with them.

4. **Final writing.** The most satisfying step in writing is preparing the final draft. It allows your student to pull together all your suggestions, and it lets the student demonstrate advanced thinking on the topic. Sometimes two or three "final" drafts must be written as the student incorporates more and more of your corrections. Do remember, though, that not all writing pieces are important enough to be polished. Encourage the student to polish only the pieces that are worth the effort.

**5. Publishing.** Put your student's writings into a booklet, or type them up into a more formal product. The student will then have something concrete and admirable to show for the lessons.

---

*Checklist Review*

**Sequence for Developing Writing Skills
with Intermediate Students**

1. Prewriting
   Presenting a stimulus
   Gathering ideas
   Clustering ideas
2. Writing
   Writing a topic sentence
   Writing the first draft
3. Revising
   Paragraph development
   Sentence structure
   Grammar basics
   Capitalization and punctuation
   Spelling
4. Final writing
5. Publishing

---

# Activities for Intermediate Writers

Personal experience is a good starting point for writing activities. Some personal experience topics can be found in Topics for Language-Experience Stories on pages 156–157. In addition, the following list suggests other activities for intermediate writers. These activities involve the writing of descriptive essays, narratives, and expository essays.

- See the activities marked with an asterisk (*) in the comprehension activities on pages 102–109.
- Ask the student to write a personal response to the reading topic.
- Have the student write a different ending to a story just read.
- The student can write a play based on a story he or she has just read.
- Have the student write a letter to "Dear Abby."
- Have the student write some questions and answers about the reading.
- You and the student can write letters to each other about books each of you has read.
- You and the student can choose between you who will be "odds" and who will be "evens." Then throw a die. If it comes up 1, 3, or 5, the "odds" person writes the first sentence to a story. Throw the die again and continue with the story.
- Write a three-word sentence. Then tell the student to rewrite the sentence, adding a word. Continue taking turns until you can't think of more to add. For example: The man worked. The old man worked. The old man worked hard. The old man worked very hard. The old man never worked very hard.
- Let your student keep a journal in which he or she writes at least twice a week. Read the journal, but don't correct it.
- Have the student write an autobiography consisting of short essays describing meaningful incidents in his or her life.
- Ask your student to write a story about someone who has had a significant (positive or negative) effect on his or her life, either as a child or as an adult. The story should start with a description of the person.
- Tell the student to take something that he or she wrote earlier and add descriptive words to the nouns or verbs in it.
- Have the student combine simple sentences into longer ones. For example: The woman is small. The woman is pretty. The woman sits on the park bench./The small, pretty woman sits on the park bench.
- The student can copy a paragraph from a reading, changing the text from one character to two characters or from the third person

singular to the third person plural or from present tense to past tense. For example: The old man has his pipe in his hand./The old men have their pipes in their hands./They have their pipes in their hands./The old man had his pipe in his hand.

■ First, have your student list ideas about how to do something. Then have him or her make the list into an outline. Finally, have the student make the outline into a narrative.

■ Have the student write for three minutes straight without lifting the pen or pencil from the page. Then try this for five minutes. Don't concern yourself with what is written, but do require that the writing be continuous.

■ Have the student write a description of something he or she knows how to do.

■ Tape-record a conversation between you and your student. Then have him or her listen to the recording and write about it.

■ Have the student interview you and then write about it.

■ Have the student write about an object one of you has brought to the tutoring session.

■ Ask the student to write a description of his or her neighborhood or work environment.

■ Let the student try writing headlines for newspaper articles.

■ The student can write a newspaper article about a current event or an event that he or she knows about.

■ Have the student write a business letter.

■ Have the student write a book of short articles, adding one new one each week.

■ Tell the student to look in the mirror and write what he or she sees.

■ Ask your student to write a story about two characters. It should start with a description of them and then tell about some interaction between them.

■ Show a picture or photo to the student and have him or her write the following about it.

—what might have come before it

—the main idea of it

—inferences that might be drawn from it

—what might have come after it

—how the people in the picture might have felt

—the relationship of the picture to his or her own feelings

—a title for it

■ Have the student write a story about the person he or she would like to be.

■ Let the student describe himself or herself, including likes and dislikes, and then write the description.

■ Ask the student to write a story about his or her favorite TV character.

■ Have the student write his or her favorite joke(s).

■ See if the student can imagine what would happen if the lights went out or if there were no food or water. Then have him or her write about it.

■ Ask the student to write what he or she would do if he or she won a lot of money.

■ Ask the student to think back to his or her best or worst day and then write what happened to make it so good or bad.

■ Have the student write what he or she would do if he or she were the last person on earth.

■ Let the student write about something he or she would like to invent.

■ Let the student try writing a short poem.

## Activities for Beginning Writers

Perhaps your student reads at the third- or fourth-grade level but is unable to write even a complete sentence. The skills-developing sequence for intermediate writers will not work for this student. What you need are simple, task-oriented, guided exercises such as the following that will build your student's self-confidence and basic writing skills.

■ Let your student write a language-experience story using the method discussed on page 156.

■ Have the student complete a partly filled-in outline of a story just read.

■ Ask the student to write a few simple sentences that you dictate; then self-correct them from your copy.

■ Have the student copy a few sentences from a story.

■ Let the student try composing endings for sentences that you begin with such phrases as, "I want to" and "I wish."

■ Ask your student to copy information from cards in his or her wallet.

■ Help the student fill in application forms.

■ See if the student can copy recipes.

■ Have the student make shopping lists.

■ You and the student can write telegrams to each other.

■ Have your student send away for something.

■ Work with the student to fill in memo pads.

■ Let the student try doing simple crossword puzzles that you make up.

■ Have your student answer a job ad.

■ Ask the student to write a letter.

■ Have the student fill in the blanks of a paragraph you have written.

■ The student can make a list of things to get done during the week.

Now use Practice Problem 3–7 to practice revising a poorly written letter.

PRACTICE PROBLEM 3–7: Writing
Suppose your student wrote the following first draft of a letter. What would you do to help the student correct errors and revise the letter into final form?

Dear Carol
I had a very nice day vizit you last week we did some nice thing. I like goin to your friend ranch most it was xcitin to ride the horse. even if I almos fall off.

Love Mike

You will find a sample solution to this practice problem on page 192.

# Sample Solutions to Practice Problems in Part 3, Chapter 3

PRACTICE PROBLEM 3–1: Sight Words
The first ten words from the basic sight-word list are listed below. Review the sight-word activities and then describe how you would use three of them with these words.

| | | |
|---|---|---|
| about | almost | am |
| after | also | an |
| again | always | and |
| all | | |

1. *Make a flash card for each of the ten words. Spread the cards on the table with the sight words facing up. Have the student find each word as I say it.*

2. *Have the student make up a sentence for each of the ten words, using the word in the sentence. Write the sentences on the backs of the cards.*

3. *Ask the student to classify the words first by the number of letters in them and then alphabetically.*

PRACTICE PROBLEM 3–2: Phonics
Read the following selection from a short story written at the third-grade level.* Then do the activities listed below the reading.

Mark Nelson sat on the park bench. It was fall. The wind blew past Mark's face. He looked up at the trees. The leaves were changing colors. The trees were a mass of orange and yellow. Mark could look at those trees for hours. At least it was something to do. He was waiting for Rita. And Rita was always late. . . .

Mark lit a cigarette. Just then, Rita walked up. "Why don't you quit smoking?" she asked Mark. Rita had quit the month before. Now she was after Mark to do the same.

*From *Looking Good* (Career Reader No. 6—Beauty Operator) by Nadine Rosenthal. David S. Lake Publishers, Belmont, Calif. (1986).

1. Find two small words with short *a* and two words with long *a*/silent *e*. List them here.

| Short *a* words | Long *a*/silent *e* words |
|---|---|
| sat | face |
| past | late |

Develop a phonics activity for one of the four words you listed above. Refer to the lists on pages 146–147.

*Brainstorm words in the family with sat: bat, cat, fat, hat, mat, pat, rat, flat, slat, brat, spat, chat, that. Write each one on a 3" x 5" card. Then drill short a.*

2. Find one word that has *ee* in it and one word that has *ea* in it. List them here.

Vowel-combination *ee* word    Vowel-combination *ea* word

trees        leaves

Develop a phonics activity for one of the vowel-combination words you noted above. Refer to the lists on pages 146–147.

*Brainstorm other ee and ea word families and then drill them. Examples: -eed, -eet, -ead, -eat.*

PRACTICE PROBLEM 3–3: Syllabication

1. Identify eight two-syllable words in this section on syllabication that adhere to the VC/CV rule. (Don't include the examples that are given.)

| | |
|---|---|
| *number* | *follows* |
| *compound* | *percent* |
| *suffix* | *letters* |
| *mastered* | *common* |

2. Develop a syllabication activity for the words noted above. Use the list on pages 152–153 to help you.

*Have the student break the words into syllables and try to figure out the rule for how to do it.*

PRACTICE PROBLEM 3–4: Language Experience

Without looking back, list the ten steps for the language-experience procedure.

*1. I choose a topic with the student.*

*2. The student dictates a story to me.*

*3. I print the story.*

*4. The student reads the story back with my help.*

*5. The student reads the story alone.*

*6. I ask the student questions about the story.*

*7. I work with the student on sight words, word families, and unknown words.*

*8. The student copies the story in a notebook.*

*9. The student corrects the story and rereads it.*

*10. I type the story for review during the next session.*

PRACTICE PROBLEM 3–5: Vocabulary Building
Read the following paragraph on beauticians,* and then find the root for each of the five words listed below. Generate more words that use the root in combination with various prefixes and suffixes.

Beauty operators, also called *beauticians, hairstylists,* or *cosmetologists,* care for customers' hair, hands, nails, and skin. They give permanents and lighten or darken the color of hair. They may give manicures and scalp and facial treatments, apply makeup, and clean and style wigs.

*From *Teacher's Guide for The Career Readers* by Nadine Rosenthal. David S. Lake Publishers, Belmont, Calif. (1986).

1. operators: *operate — operation, operating, operated, operative, inoperable*

2. beauticians: *beauty — beau, beautiful, beautify, beauteous*

3. cosmetologists: *cosmetic — cosmetology, cosmetician*

4. manicures: *cure — pedicure, cured, curing, cure-all, curator, curative, incurable*

5. facial: *face — facing, faced, faceless, face-saving, facade, face value*

PRACTICE PROBLEM 3–6: SPELLING
1. List three words that follow each of the four spelling rules discussed in this section.

The doubling rule

*clap/clapping   swim/swimmer   drop/dropped*

The final *e* rule

*joke/joking   like/likable   hike/hiker*

The *y* to *i* rule

*fancy / fanciful   lovely / loveliest   happy / happiness*

The *ie-ei* rule

*conceive*          *retrieve*          *fierce*

2. Without looking back, list the ten steps in the flash-card spelling technique.

1. I make a flash card for each problem word.

2. The student looks at the card and says the word slowly, listening to it.

3. The student spells the word aloud while looking at it.

4. The student spells the word aloud without looking at it.

5. The student looks at the card to correct any misspelling.

6. The student writes the word without looking at it.

7. The student looks at the card again to correct any misspelling.

8. After 3 written misspellings, I put the card aside for later drill.

9. I pick a new word. This time, the student traces it while spelling it aloud.

10. I throw out the card for a word written correctly 3 times.

PRACTICE PROBLEM 3–7: Writing

Suppose your student wrote the following first draft of a letter. What would you do to help the student correct errors and revise the letter into final form?

Dear Carol

I had a very nice day vizit you last week we did some nice thing. I like goin to your friend ranch most it was xcitin to ride the horse. even if I almos fall off.

Love Mike

1. Tell Mike to add a comma after the opening in a letter and after the word or words used before his name in the closing.
2. Begin teaching Mike about sentence structure. Show him examples in his letter of run-on and incomplete sentences.
3. Teach Mike how to spell visit, exciting, and almost. Add them to his list of words to learn.
4. Teach Mike about -ing endings, as in going and exciting.
5. Leave the rest alone. Later, perhaps, we'll work on some of the other problems.

# PART 4

# *Teaching Resources*

# National Literacy Contact Number

The national literacy contact phone number is 800-228-8813. This toll-free number has the names, addresses, and telephone numbers of 6,400 adult literacy programs. It also provides free information on literacy and on literacy programs. The organization that operates the number is

CONTACT Literacy Center
(a division of Contact, Inc.)
P. O. Box 81826
Lincoln, NB 68501

CONTACT Literacy Center is one of 11 nonprofit organizations that promote literacy under the umbrella of the

Coalition for Literacy
American Library Association
50 East Huron Street
Chicago, IL 60611

# Publishers of High-Interest, Low-Level Books for Adults and Adolescents

Send postcards requesting the adult basic education or new readers catalog.

Bay Area Writing Project
University of California
Tolman Hall
Berkeley, CA 94720

Bookwise Marketing, Inc.
235 Willamette Avenue
Kensington, CA 94708

Cambridge Publishers
888 Seventh Avenue
New York, NY 10106

David S. Lake Publishers
Fearon Education Division
19 Davis Drive
Belmont, CA 94002

Educators Publishing Service
75 Moulton Street
Cambridge, MA 02238

Follett Publishing Co.
1010 Washington Boulevard
Chicago, IL 60607

Frank E. Richards Publishing
P. O. Box 66
Phoenix, AZ 13135

Globe Book Company, Inc.
50 West 23rd Street
New York, NY 10010

Jamestown Publishers
P. O. Box 6743
Providence, RI 02940

Janus Book Publishers
2501 Industrial Parkway West
Hayward, CA 94545

Learnco, Inc.
128 High Street
Greenland, NH 03840

Literacy Volunteers of America
404 Oak Street
Syracuse, NY 13203

McGraw-Hill Book Company
Adult Education Services S1
Hightstown/Princeton Road
Hightstown, NJ 08520

Midwest Publications
P. O. Box 448
Pacific Grove, CA 93950

New Readers Press
Laubach Literacy
Box 131
Syracuse, NY 13210

Scott, Foresman Publishers
Lifelong Learning Division
1900 East Lake Avenue
Glenview, IL 60025

Steck-Vaughn Company
P. O. Box 2028
Austin, TX 78768

# Reference Materials on Adult Literacy and Reading

Ashton-Warner, Sylvia. *Teacher.* Matrix Series. New York: Bantam, 1971.

Bettelheim, Bruno, and Zelan, Karen. *On Learning to Read: The Child's Fascination with Meaning.* New York: Random House, 1983.

Copperman, Paul. *The Literacy Hoax: The Decline of Reading, Writing, and Learning in the Public Schools and What We Can Do About It.* New York: Morrow, 1978.

Costello, William. "How Can I Help My Child Learn to Read?" *Instructor* (Nov./Dec., 1984): 72–74.

DeStefano, Johanna S. *Language, the Learner, and the School.* New York: Wiley, 1978.

Dettre, Judith H. *1, 2, 3, Read!* Belmont, Calif.: David S. Lake Publishers, 1980.

Fader, Daniel. *The New Hooked on Books.* New York: Berkley Publishing, 1983.

Freire, Paolo. *Pedagogy of the Oppressed.* Translated by Myra B. Ramos. New York: Continuum Publishing, 1970.

Hart, Leslie A. *Human Brain and Human Learning.* New York: Longman, 1983.

Heilman, Arthur W. *Phonics in Proper Perspective.* 4th ed. Columbus, Ohio: Charles E. Merrill Publishing, 1981.

Howards, Melvin. *Reading Diagnosis and Instruction: An Integrated Approach.* Reston, Va.: Reston Publishing, 1980.

Kozol, Jonathan. *Prisoners of Silence: Breaking the Bonds of Adult Illiteracy in the United States.* New York: Continuum Publishing, 1980.

Kozol, Jonathan. *Illiterate America.* New York: Doubleday, 1985.

Shaughnessy, Mina. *Errors and Expectations: A Guide for the Teacher of Basic Writing.* New York: Oxford University Press, 1977.

Shor, Ira. *Critical Teaching and Everyday Life.* Boston: South End Press, 1980.

Smith, Frank. *Reading Without Nonsense.* New York: Teachers College Press, 1979.

Strong, William. *Sentence Combining: A Composing Book.* New York: Random House, 1973.

Trela, Thaddeus M. *Fourteen Remedial Reading Methods.* Belmont, Calif.: David S. Lake Publishers, 1967.

Trelease, James. *The Read-Aloud Handbook.* Wheaton, Ill.: Tyndale House Publishers, 1982.

Wallerstein, Nina. *Language and Culture in Conflict.* Reading, Mass.: Addison-Wesley Publishing, 1983.

# Checklist Reviews from Part 3, Chapter 2

---

*Checklist Review*

## Selecting Reading Topics and Materials

1. Decide on a topic with your student, either by selecting one of obvious interest to him or her or by using the Reading Topics List.

2. Find appropriate reading materials on that topic; or write down materials to the student's reading level; or create materials by writing your own stories.

3. Expand the reading topic when necessary by brainstorming and building activities flowcharts.

---

*Checklist Review*

## Questioning Pattern

Literal Recall Questions
*Describe* = Describe the content of the reading.
*Reorganize* = Reorganize the reading into your own words.

Interpretive Questions
*Analyze* = Analyze the ideas from the reading.
*Generalize* = to larger issues.

Active Questions
*React* = React emotionally to the reading.
*Act* = Act on your thoughts and feelings about the reading.

## Checklist Review

### Active Questioning Training

1. Read a sentence or paragraph.
2. Ask a broad question about it.
3. Decide if the answer can be found in the text or if you must figure it out.
4. Find or figure out the answer.
5. Explain your line of reasoning.
6. Go on to the next sentence or paragraph.

### Active Clarifying Training

1. Read a sentence or paragraph.
2. Put your thumb up if you understand it. Then continue reading.
3. Put your thumb down if you don't understand it.
4. Decide if the problem is with a word, a phrase, or with the whole thing.
5. Reread and discuss the reading to clarify the difficult parts.
6. Go on to the next sentence or paragraph.

### Active Remembering Training

1. Read a sentence or paragraph.
2. Summarize it.
3. Decide what is important to remember.
4. Predict what will come next.
5. Go on to the next sentence or paragraph.
6. Summarize all of what you've read.

| *Checklist Review* |
| --- |
| SQ3R Study Skills Technique |

| | |
| --- | --- |
| S = Survey | Survey the reading as a whole or by section. |
| Q = Question | Change each heading and subheading into a question. |
| R = Reading | Read the material under each heading and subheading to answer the question. |
| R = Recite | Recite the information and ideas learned under each heading and subheading. |
| R = Review | Review the reading as a whole. |

# Checklist Reviews from Part 3, Chapter 3

| *Checklist Review* |
| --- |
| Phonics Sequence |

1. Single consonants
2. Short vowels
3. Beginning blends
4. End blends
5. Beginning and end digraphs
6. Long vowels with silent *e*
7. Long vowels in two-vowel combinations
8. Miscellaneous vowel combinations
9. Vowels controlled by *r, l,* and *w*
10. Contractions

---

*Checklist Review*

## Syllabication Rules

1. Compound words: some/day
2. V̆C/CV: pen/cil
3. V̄/CV or V̆C/V: ho/tel or lem/on
4. Words ending in *le:* sam/ple
5. Prefixes and endings: un/sure and sure/ly
6. Blends and digraphs: con/trol and fash/ion

---

*Checklist Review*

## Language-Experience Procedure

1. Choose a topic with your student.
2. The student dictates a story to you.
3. You print the story.
4. Your student reads the story back with your help.
5. The student reads the story alone.
6. You ask the student questions about the story.
7. You work with the student on sight words, word families, and unknown words from the story.
8. The student copies the story in a notebook.
9. The student corrects the story and rereads it.
10. You type the story for review during the next session.

---

*Checklist Review*

## Vocabulary-Building Methods

1. Building word lists
2. Finding word origins
3. Analyzing prefixes and roots
4. Developing the dictionary habit
5. Getting familiar with the thesaurus
6. Using the frontier system

---

*Checklist Review*

## Sources of Spelling Words

1. Word families
2. Sight words
3. Topic words
4. Homonyms
5. Spelling rules

---

*Checklist Review*

## Sequence for Developing Writing Skills with Intermediate Students

1. Prewriting
   Presenting a stimulus
   Gathering ideas
   Clustering ideas

2. Writing
   Writing a topic sentence
   Writing the first draft

3. Revising
   Paragraph development
   Sentence structure
   Grammar basics
   Capitalization and punctuation
   Spelling

4. Final writing

5. Publishing

# Nonstandard English

Nonstandard English develops from geographic isolation rather than from language deprivation. It comprises various complete languages, each with pronunciation and syntax rules that are different from but similar to standard English. The difficulty with using a nonstandard language is that most people speak, understand, and write standard English in order to be able to communicate with each other. Children who speak a nonstandard language often feel inferior or angry if they are not respected by their teachers and peers for their language or intelligence. Feelings of inferiority and anger can play a large role in inhibiting learning.

Should the reading tutor teach standard English to a student who speaks nonstandard English? You must be careful not to confuse variances in speech with reading problems. Remember, literacy means taking *meaning* from print and giving meaning to print. It matters little whether your student drops endings or uses nonstandard verb forms when reading aloud if he or she understands the meaning of the words. On the other hand, a student may wish to speak and write standard English in addition to his or her nonstandard language. This will allow the student to communicate in the language of the larger society and thus succeed in it. If this is the case with your student, devote a part of your lessons to teaching standard English grammar and syntax.

Before beginning this process, it will be helpful to understand some of the rules of Black English, a widespread nonstandard English language. You can find books and articles on Black English and nonstandard English in your library that will give you more information. But the few generalizations below on how Black English pronunciation and syntax differ from standard English can be useful.

- Using simplified endings; for example, don't/don, hold/hol, finding/findin, laughed/laugh
- Substitution of *f* for *th*; for example, mouth/mouf, path/paf
- Substitution of *them* for *those* and *they* for *their*; for example, give me those books/give me them books, they left their books/ they left they books.

- Substitution of *be* for *is* and *are* as a helping verb; for example, she is walking/she be walking, they are coming/they be coming.
- Using double negatives; for example, I don't have any money/I ain't got no money.

225-N